Junk Drawer

GEOMETRY

50 AWESOME ACTIVITIES | That Don't Cost a Thing

BOBBY MERCER

CHICAGO
REVIEW
PRESS

Library of Congress Cataloging-in-Publication Data
Names: Mercer, Bobby, 1961– author.
Title: Junk drawer geometry : 50 awesome activities that don't cost a thing /
    Bobby Mercer.
Description: Chicago, Illinois : Chicago Review Press Incorporated, [2018] |
    Audience: Ages 9+ | Audience: Grades 4 to 6. | Includes index.
Identifiers: LCCN 2018009570 (print) | LCCN 2018012280 (ebook) | ISBN
    9780912777801 (adobe pdf) | ISBN 9780912777818 (epub) | ISBN 9780912777825
    (kindle) | ISBN 9780912777795 (trade paper)
Subjects: LCSH: Geometrical constructions—Juvenile literature. |
    Geometry—Juvenile literature. | Mathematical recreations—Juvenile
    literature.
Classification: LCC QA445.5 (ebook) | LCC QA445.5 .M465 2018 (print) | DDC
    516.0078—dc23
LC record available at https://lccn.loc.gov/2018009570

Cover design: Andrew Brozyna
Interior design: Jonathan Hahn
Photo credits: Bobby Mercer

Printed in the United States of America
5 4 3 2 1

To Jennifer, Leslie, Laura, Ethan, and Shannon.
Thanks for always being there.

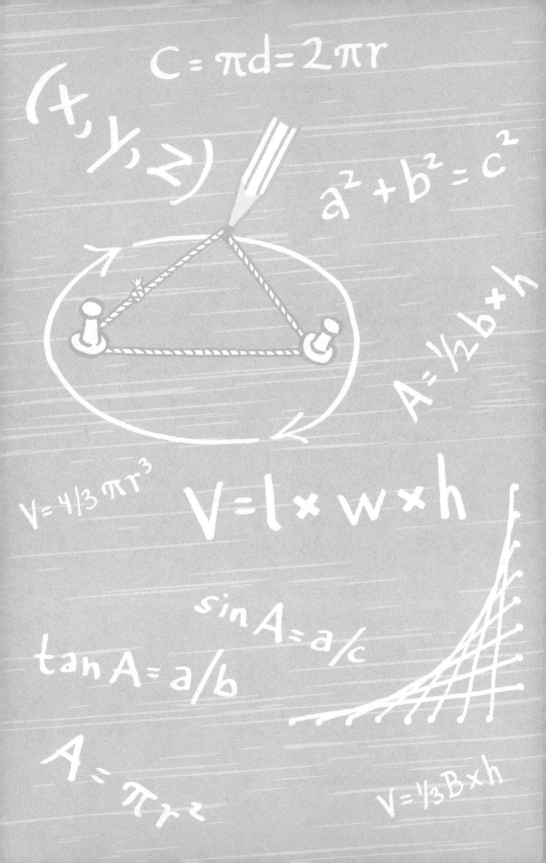

Contents

Acknowledgments

B ooks don't happen without great people helping along the way. Thanks to Kathy Green, the best agent in the business. Thanks to Jerome Pohlen and the gifted people at Chicago Review Press for having the courage to publish a math book for everybody. Thanks to the wonderful people I work with; their thoughts, ideas, and encouragement mean the world to me. Jon Ezell, Caitlin Williams, Hunter Allen, Doug Campbell, and Kristen Korzelius gave me math inspiration. Team Science—Shannon Haynes, Jennifer Allsbrook, Ethan Abbott, and Leslie Rhinehart—have been invaluable as shoulders to lean on. As always, thanks to my wonderful better half, Michele, and my two partners in hands-on mayhem, Nicole and Jordan.

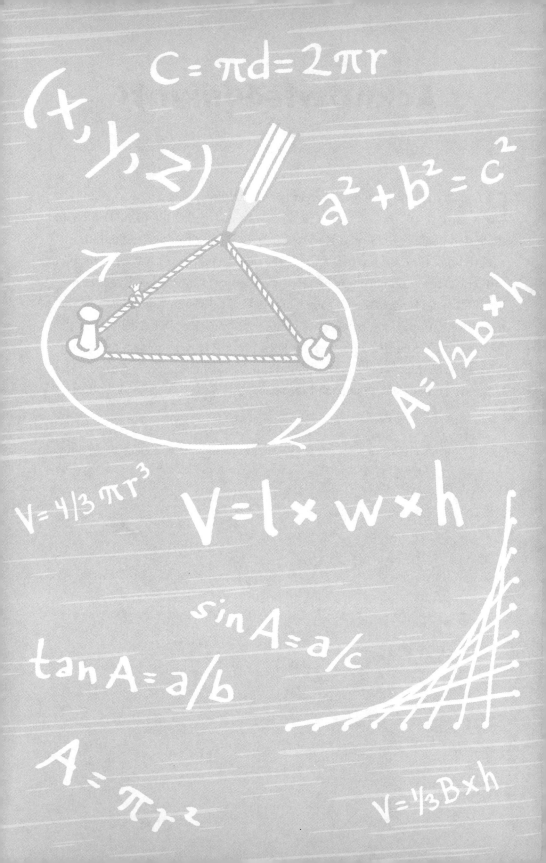

Introduction

M ath is easy for some and hard for others. If math is easy, the sky's the limit for career choices. Many of the top fields for students now involve STEM—Science, Technology, Engineering, and Math. Math truly is a key that can unlock many doors to further a young person's education.

As a lifelong science teacher, I understand that math is the language of physics and chemistry. Also, science is based on hands-on inquiry learning. Students learn better if they can touch or see a concept in action. Many of the activities in this book were developed to help students better grasp geometry concepts. My high school students always struggle with what a radian is until they try the "Radians Are Fun" activity. It's easier to understand when they can see it. Each activity also contains a section called "Math for the Ages." This section will give hints on how to modify activities for different age groups.

An early love of math will lead to higher test scores, but more important, it leads to a greater understanding of math. And understanding math helps develop critical thinking skills that transcend subjects. Good musicians usually *get* math. Good doctors *get* math.

One thing I have always tried to do is show students the fun of math and science. Some activities are designed for teachers or parents to simply reach students. If students smile about a subject, they are more likely to want to learn. To teach a student, you have to reach the student. Have fun, enjoy these activities, and use them as a stepping stone toward math mastery.

Math takes practice. And a great way to see this practice is with an introductory activity.

Student Whiteboards

Make your own set of classroom whiteboards for under $20.

Adult supervision required

From the Junk Drawer:

☐ Sheet of white bathroom wall   ☐ Power saw
    paneling   ☐ Sandpaper (optional)

Step 1: Visit your local home improvement store and buy one (or two) sheets of white bathroom wall paneling. Many home improvement stores are set up to cut panels for you. If a sales assistant won't cut the whole panel for you, they may be willing to split it in half for you, which will make it easier to get the paneling home. Another option is to ask if the store has any broken panels. Oftentimes one corner of a panel is damaged and the store will sell it at a discount. Once you're home, cut the paneling into 12-by-16-inch **rectangles** (making 24 whiteboards per sheet) or 12-by-24-inch rectangles (16 whiteboards per sheet). The paneling can be cut with a normal power saw and blade. If you are a high school or middle school teacher and your school teaches carpentry or woodshop, they will likely be glad to cut it if you ask. Once the panels are cut, you can use sandpaper to smooth any sharp edges.

The Math Behind It

Giving students individual whiteboards is a cheap and easy way to let them write, calculate, and fix mistakes easily using dry-erase markers. It also makes classroom monitoring of how students are learning easier because you can easily see each student's work. Plus, kids love drawing on them.

Giving whiteboards to my students might be the best thing I ever did in my teaching career. I created a set 20 years ago that I still use today, either individually or in pairs, at least twice a week. The dry-erase ink cleans easily with paper towels, though I now have a shoebox full of erasers for students to use.

You can buy whiteboards, but two boards from a store will cost you more than an entire panel of bathroom paneling. For homeschooling, buying a single board may be the way to go. Store-bought whiteboards have one advantage in that they usually have a metal backing that makes them magnetic and easy to mount on walls.

Math for the Ages

The boards are a hit with all ages. Since they're small and portable, they are great for car trips or for math or science practice.

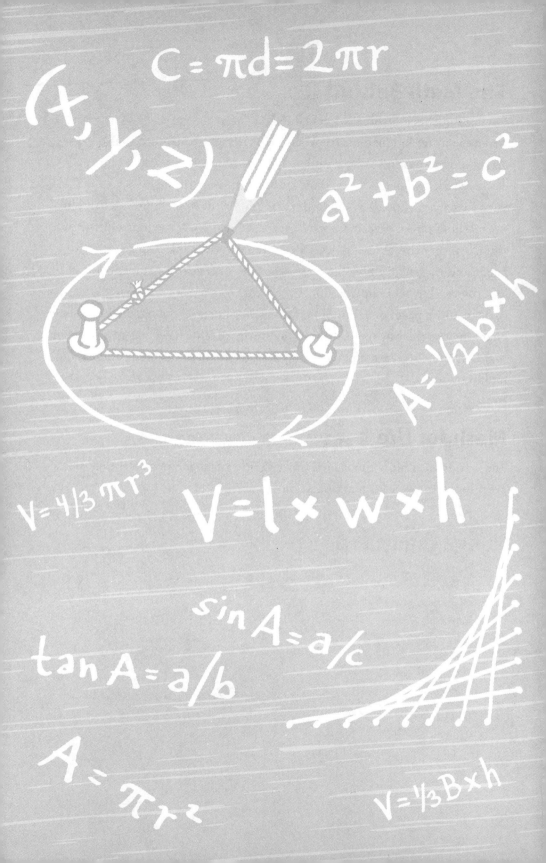

Geometry Tools

Geometry naturally lends itself to fun tools. **Compasses**, protractors, and rulers, just to name a few, are staples in math classrooms. Traditional math tools are important, and there are easy, inexpensive ways for students to make some of their own tools. You can also create some new tools out of everyday objects.

Math is not a spectator sport; it should be experienced. People understand math better when they touch it. So let's make some tools to help us learn geometry.

Pencil Compass

Use two pencils, rubber bands, and scrap cardboard to create perfect small **circles**.

Geometry Concepts: Compasses, circles, **radius**, and **diameter**

From the Junk Drawer:

- ☐ 2 sharpened pencils
- ☐ 2 rubber bands
- ☐ Scissors
- ☐ Scrap corrugated cardboard
- ☐ Scrap paper
- ☐ Pushpin or thumbtack

Step 1: Wrap a rubber band several times around the eraser end of two sharpened pencils that are the same length, binding the pencils together. You should be able to pull the sharpened ends of the pencils apart.

Step 2: Cut a piece of scrap corrugated cardboard approximately ½ inch wide by 1½ inches long. Cut a small *v* out of each short end of the scrap as shown.

Step 3: Slide the notched cardboard between the two pencils. The rubber band should be loose enough that you can move the cardboard up and down. Loosen or tighten the rubber band as needed.

Step 4: Wrap the second rubber band around the two pencils directly below the notched cardboard piece. This rubber band will keep the cardboard from sliding. Your compass is ready to use now.

Step 5: Place a sheet of paper on top of a larger scrap of corrugated cardboard. Use a pushpin or thumbtack to punch a small hole through the paper and cardboard. Put one pencil point in this hole—you want this pencil to remain in place. Hold the top of your Pencil Compass with one hand, then use your other hand to spin the second pencil 360 degrees to draw a circle.

Step 6: Move the notched cardboard piece up or down between the pencils to create different-sized circles. With practice, you can stop using the pushpin and the scrap cardboard under the paper and draw simple circles all day long with your Pencil Compass.

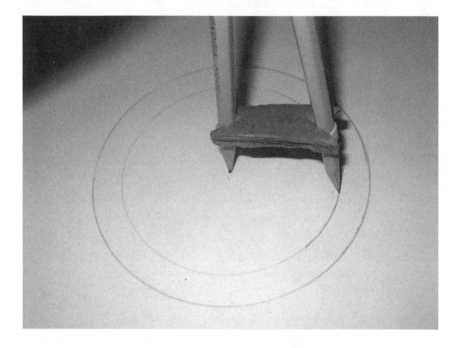

The Math Behind It

Compasses are one of the most useful tools around (pun intended). Compasses allow you to draw circles. Store-bought compasses are a staple in most math classes, but there are several ways to make your own. The distance between the two pencil points is the radius of your circle. The diameter is the complete width of your circle.

Math for the Ages

This activity is suitable for all ages. Younger students should use the scrap corrugated cardboard beneath the paper when drawing circles to help steady their hands.

World's Simplest Compass

A strip of paper, a pencil, and a thumbtack are all you need to draw circles.

Geometry Concepts: **Concentric circles**, radius, and diameter

From the Junk Drawer:

- ☐ Strip of heavy paper (like old holiday cards or recycled magazine covers)
- ☐ Thumbtack or pushpin
- ☐ Scrap corrugated cardboard
- ☐ Ruler
- ☐ Pencil

Step 1: Cut a 1-by-6-inch strip of heavy paper. Use a thumbtack or pushpin to poke a hole through one end of the paper. The hole should be centered. Mark that point *C* for center with a pencil.

Step 2: Using a ruler, mark every inch from the hole to the other end of the paper, as shown. At each mark use the thumbtack to poke a hole big enough for the pencil's lead to go through.

Step 3: Put your sheet of paper on top of the corrugated cardboard. Push the thumbtack through the C point and leave the tack in, but loose enough so the paper spins. This is your compass! Place your pencil lead through one of the holes and simply spin it (and the paper with it) around to draw a circle.

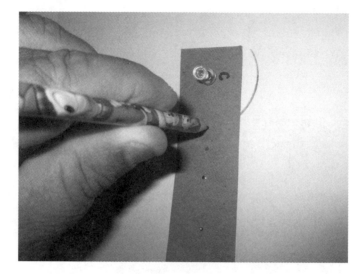

Step 4: Try drawing a bigger or smaller circle by putting your pencil in a new hole. The circles you draw are called concentric circles.

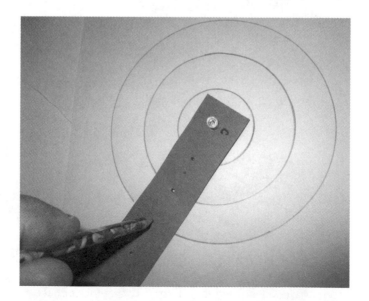

The Math Behind It

Concentric circles are circles with a common center and different **radii**. The distance from the center hole to the hole with the pencil lead is the radius of the circle. The diameter is the entire distance across the circle, or twice the radius.

Math for the Ages

This is a safe activity for all ages, especially if you use pushpins. Another option is to have elementary and middle school students draw six different-sized circles and then calculate the **area** of each. Middle and high school students could graph area on the y-axis and radius on the x-axis for each circle they drew. The shape of the graph will be a **parabola**, which reinforces that area equals pi times the radius of a circle squared ($A = \pi \times r^2$).

Magnetic Triangle Flash Cards

Create large **triangles** of all the different types—**equilateral, isosceles, scalene, acute, obtuse**, and **right**—for Triangle Flash Cards.

Geometry Concepts: Different types of triangles

From the Junk Drawer:

☐ Scissors
☐ Old cereal boxes, file folders, or construction paper
☐ Marker
☐ Glue or glue sticks
☐ Magnets or magnet tape
☐ Magnetic surface

Step 1: Use scissors to cut out different types of triangles from old cereal boxes, file folders, or construction paper. Write the type of triangle on one side with a marker. The common types of triangles are:

Equilateral: each side equal length (and all **angles** equal)
Isosceles: two sides equal length (and two angles equal)

Scalene: all sides of different lengths

Right: one 90-degree angle

Acute: all angles less than 90 degrees

Obtuse: one angle greater than 90 degrees

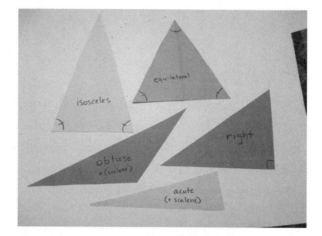

Step 2: Use glue to affix a magnet to the back of each triangle. (To hide the magnets, you can cut a small **square** of the triangle material and cover the magnet with another dab of glue.) You can use almost any old magnet piece, or you can buy magnetic tape in the craft section at most big-box and dollar stores. You only need a small piece, so a roll will go a long way.

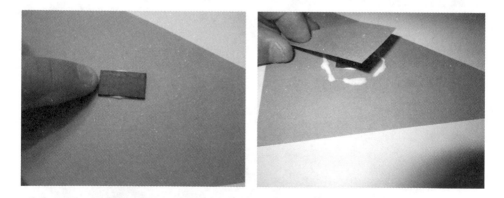

Step 3: Place the triangles with the writing side down on any magnetic surface, such as a refrigerator, filing cabinet, or whiteboard. Quiz yourself

or friends on the definition and name of each triangle, then flip them over to see if you're right.

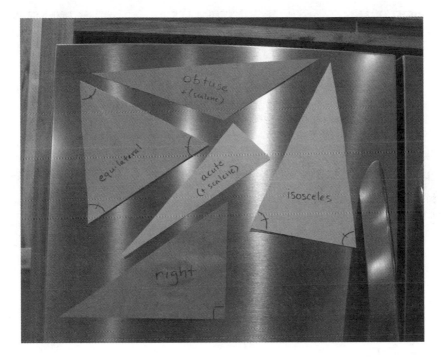

The Math Behind It

All triangles have three sides, but they are classified based on their angles and side lengths. Equilateral triangles have three equal sides and three equal angles. Isosceles triangles have two equal sides and two equal angles. Isosceles triangles can also be acute, obtuse, or right triangles, depending on their angles (see below). Scalene triangles have three different angles and three different side lengths.

Right triangles have one angle that is equal to 90 degrees. A right triangle is also classified as an isosceles triangle if the other two angles are 45 degrees each. Acute triangles have three different angles, all less than 90 degrees. Acute triangles can be right, isosceles, or scalene. Obtuse triangles have three different angles, but one angle is greater than 90 degrees. They can be isosceles or scalene, depending on the length of their sides.

This table summarizes the overlap of different types of triangles:

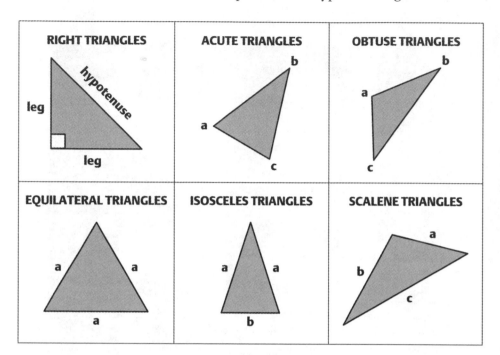

Math for the Ages

Triangles are taught to young children, so this activity is appropriate for almost all ages. And if children learn this at home, they will have a head start when they see it in school. In a classroom setting, you could have groups of students make sets of these magnetized triangles and then place them wherever they'll stick in the classroom. The students can quiz themselves or one another on the different types. This interactive activity gets students out of their seats for a few minutes. Research shows that students perform better when learning is interspersed with physical activity.

For older children, you could label two angle measurements on one side of each triangle with the actual number of degrees. Have the students calculate the missing angle. The interior angles of any triangle add up to 180 degrees. This activity extension would be a great way to practice and apply this fact.

Straw Polygon

Make a convertible **polygon**.

Geometry Concepts: Quadrilaterals, squares, rectangles, rhombuses, **trapezoids**, and **parallelograms**

From the Junk Drawer:

☐ Scissors

☐ Two pipe cleaners

☐ Four flexible drinking straws

☐ Glue (optional)

Step 1: Use your scissors to cut your two pipe cleaners in half, making four pieces. These pieces will be the corners of your Straw Polygons. Slide one pipe cleaner piece halfway inside one of your straws. Slide another straw onto the other end of the same pipe cleaner. Leave a small piece of the pipe cleaner exposed to be able to bend into a corner. Repeat for the remaining two straws.

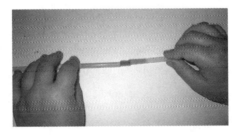

Step 2: Bend one of the straw-pipe cleaner combinations to a 90-degree angle at the joint where the two straws meet. Repeat for the other straw–pipe cleaner combination.

Step 3: Slide a cut piece of pipe cleaner into the open end of one of the already bent straws. Make sure to leave half of the pipe cleaner sticking out of the straw. Now bend the pipe cleaner at 90 degrees. Slide the other combination on the other end of the pipe cleaner. Three of your four straws should now be connected.

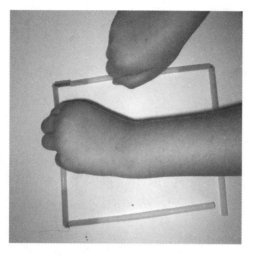

Step 4: Bend the last pipe cleaner piece at 90 degrees. Use this piece to make the fourth corner, so all of the straws are connected. With all four sides equal in length and all four angles at 90 degrees, you have a square. By changing angles, you can use the Straw Polygon to show almost all of the four-sided polygons.

Step 5 (optional): If the square is loose or you want a more permanent Straw Polygon, use any glue suitable for plastic. Pull one end of the pipe cleaner piece out of its straw and put glue onto it. Immediately slide it back into the straw. Repeat for all the other corners. Let the Straw Polygon dry completely before continuing to Step 6.

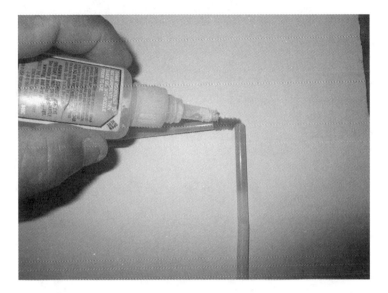

Step 6: Grab opposite corners of your Straw Polygon and gently tug. You now have a **rhombus**, which is just a lopsided square.

Step 7: Using two hands, stretch out the flexible part of one straw completely, then do the same for the straw on the opposite side. It is OK if the pipe cleaner comes out—just slide it back in. With the angles the same as your rhombus, you now have a parallelogram.

Step 8: Bend all four corners back to 90 degrees and you have a rectangle.

Step 9: Using two hands, slide only the top flexible straw pieces together. If the bottom angles are equal, you have a trapezoid.

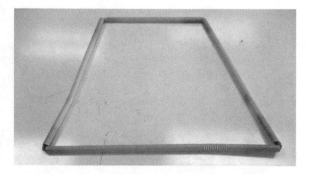

Step 10: Though it's harder, by squeezing the flexible parts of the straws to different lengths and making the four inside angles different, you can make a **quadrilateral**, where no sides or angles are equal. You could also use the scissors to change the lengths of the straws if the Straw Polygon is not glued together.

The Math Behind It

Any four-sided shape is a quadrilateral, so all of the shapes you made are quadrilaterals. But quadrilaterals can be further divided into subtypes. A square is the first quadrilateral students learn about, containing four equal sides and four equal angles. A rhombus is a tilted square, with four equal-length sides and equal opposite angles. A stretched-out rhombus with two sets of equal length sides that are parallel is a parallelogram. A special parallelogram is the familiar rectangle—it has four right angles. One set of parallel sides means you have a trapezoid. Quadrilaterals come in many shapes and sizes.

Math for the Ages

The Straw Polygon is an activity for all ages. Younger children may need supervision while cutting, and help with the glue, if you choose to use it.

Parallel Lines

Draw perfect **parallel lines** using two books.

Geometry Concepts: Parallel **lines**, perpendicular lines

From the Junk Drawer:

☐ 2 books (or any objects with straight ☐ Scrap paper
   lines, like scrap cardboard)   ☐ Pencil

Step 1: Lay one book down on a piece of paper. (You could also use a straight piece of cardboard, like a shoebox lid, or any very straight and hard piece of plastic. You can even use notebooks.) Place the second book with its edge firmly against the first at a 90-degree angle, as shown. The edge of the second book will be **perpendicular** to the first. Use a pencil to draw a line along the edge of the second book.

Step 2: Slide the second book down the edge of the first and draw another line. The line is perfectly parallel to the first. Slide and repeat as many times as you want.

The Math Behind It

This is actually an old drafting trick using plastic drafting triangles, but you can do it with stuff from your junk drawer.

Parallel lines will never cross. They would go one forever without crossing. The edges of wood flooring and floor tiles are a great place to see parallel lines. The walls of most rooms are also parallel. The lines on notebook paper are one of the best places to see parallel lines at home or school.

Two (or more) perpendicular lines drawn from a single other line will always be parallel to one another.

Math for the Ages

This activity is great for all ages and is a wonderful way to introduce the terms *parallel* and *perpendicular* to younger children. High school students would benefit from doing this, even if it only takes them two minutes. This is a great activity to fill the last few minutes of class before the bell rings. And high school students draw parallel lines in **graphing** functions, statistics, and geometric translations.

Paper Protractor

Learn the most common **angles** as you build a simple Paper Protractor.

Geometry Concept: Common angles

From the Junk Drawer:

- ☐ 8½-by-8½-inch piece of paper
- ☐ Scissors (optional)
- ☐ Pen or marker
- ☐ Protractor (optional)

Step 1: Fold your square piece of paper in half. (If you have trouble finding a perfectly square piece of paper, you can cut one yourself with scissors.) Crease the folded edge.

Step 2: Use your pen or marker to draw a dashed line along the fold. Turn the paper so that the center fold is vertical and unfold the paper. Then fold the bottom right-hand corner up until it reaches the creased fold line, with the new fold leading down directly to the lower left corner, as shown. Crease the folded edge down.

Step 3: This is the hardest step to visualize, so take your time. Rotate the paper clockwise until the lower left corner points up. Then fold the bottom up until it aligns with the bottom of your previous fold, as shown. Crease in place.

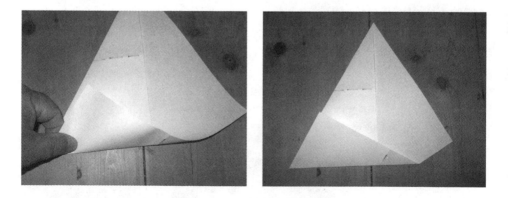

Step 4: Unfold the paper. The tri-folded angles are all exactly 60 degrees. You can mark the edges with a pen or a marker. If you want to verify the angles,

check them with a protractor. This activity proves that a straight line is an angle of 180 degrees, since 3 × 60 = 180.

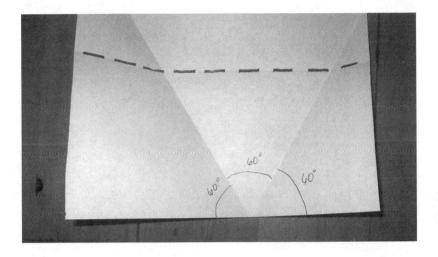

Step 5: Refold the paper and tuck the bottom triangle underneath the left flap. With a pen or marker, write *30 degrees* on both sides of the folded paper on the top. The left triangle is a 30-60-90 degree triangle, so mark the angles as shown in the picture. It is common to draw a rectangle to represent a 90-degree angle.

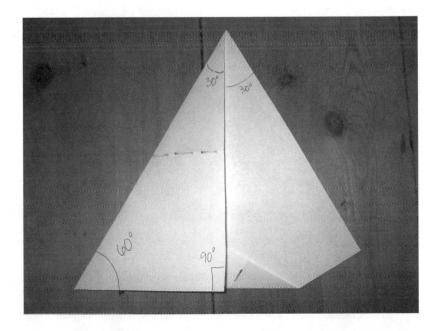

Step 6: Fold the right triangle flap in half. Crease this line down. The right triangle will be a 15-75-90 degree right triangle.

Step 7: Label the *entire* top angle *45 degrees*. Label the smaller right triangle *15 degrees*. This leftmost bottom angle of the skinnier triangle on the right is a right triangle, so label that angle *90 degrees*. All triangles have three angles that add up to 180 degrees, so simple math tells us that the lower right angle must be 75 degrees because we already know one angle is 15 degrees and the other is 90 degrees. For a fun option, you can check all of the angles with a protractor. With practice, these angles will be perfect, although they might not be the first time.

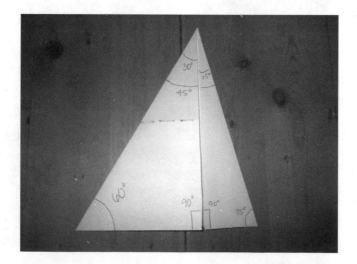

Step 8: Unfold the right triangle. The bottom angle will be 150 degrees, and you can label it with a pen.

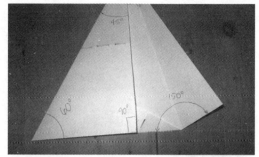

Step 9: Unfold the left triangle. The bottom angle will be 120 degrees (two 60 degree triangles together). Label it with a pen.

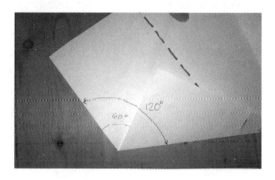

The Math Behind It

Protractors are designed to measure angles. The Paper Protractor will not allow you to measure angles directly; but it will cover most of the common angles that you encounter. The Paper Protractor is also a great way to reinforce that angles on a straight line must always add up to 180 degrees and all triangles have three angles that add up to 180 degrees.

Math for the Ages

This activity is appropriate for almost all ages. It is a great way to introduce angles and let the concept sink in. The more experience children get with angles, the better they can estimate angles; estimation will be a great way to check problems as they get older. If they understand what a 60-degree angle is, they will later solve complicated angle problems more easily. This is a short, fun activity that gives students a break from "doing math"—they will be doing math without even knowing it.

If you have older students who are familiar with geometry **theorems**, they could prove the angles by measuring the sides and using a few geometry facts.

Cubic Cardboard Boxes

Turn a rectangle cereal box into a **cube**. It will hold the same amount of cereal but use less cardboard.

Geometry Concepts: **Volume**, **rectangular prisms**, and cubes

From the Junk Drawer:

☐ Ruler

☐ Empty cereal box

☐ Scientific calculator or computer with internet access

☐ Tape

☐ Uncooked rice, dried beans, or packing peanuts (optional)

☐ Scissors

☐ Marker

Step 1: Use your ruler to measure the length, width, and height of an empty cereal box in centimeters. (Measuring in centimeters is best since you can easily measure to the nearest tenth of a centimeter. If you measure in inches, you will have to convert the fractions of inches into decimals to multiply.) Then calculate the volume of the cereal box by multiplying the length (a), width (b), and height (c). $V = a \times b \times c$.

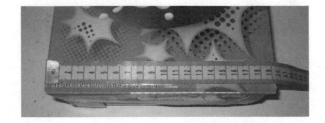

Step 2: Use a scientific calculator to find the cube root of the volume. The button usually includes the square root symbol ($\sqrt{}$) and looks similar to this: y√x. You can always have a math teacher or guardian help you with this step if needed. If you don't have a scientific calculator, you can search for "cube root of ___" (inserting your number) at Google. This is the simplest method—Google can solve virtually any math problem.

Step 3 (optional): You might want to fill your empty cereal box with uncooked rice, dried beans, or packing peanuts (the cheapest method). Fill the box completely and then pour the rice, beans, or peanuts out of the box and into a clean bowl and set aside. (Don't use the cereal from the box. Cereal is packed in air to keep it from being crushed, so it won't fill the box entirely.)

Step 4: Open both ends of the cereal box and use scissors to cut one long edge so the cardboard can lie flat. Using a marker and rule, draw six large squares on the inside of your cereal box. The length of each square's side should be the number you calculated in Step 2 (the cube root of the box's volume). Use the straight edges of the box as guiding lines when possible.

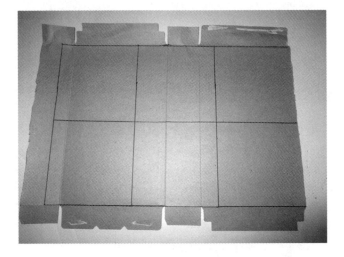

Step 5: Cut along the center line and around the leftover flaps so you have two pieces of cardboard with three squares on each piece. Use a counter or table to bend each piece of cardboard into a 90-degree angle at the lines you've drawn. When you're done, both pieces of cardboard should look like a square that's missing one side.

Step 6: Build a cube by interlocking the two bent pieces of cardboard and securing the edges with tape. If you want to do the optional Step 7, leave one side untaped like a lid.

Step 7 (optional): If you did Step 3, pour the rice, beans, or packing peanuts back into the cube to see if it has the same volume. Does it? Now look at all the cardboard scraps left over. Ask yourself: *Why aren't the boxes shaped like cubes to save cardboard?*

The Math Behind It

Cereal boxes are a shape called a rectangular prism. Rectangles are flat; since our cereal box is three dimensional, it is referred to as a rectangular prism. Cereal companies could save money by making **cubic** boxes, since cubes require less material than rectangles to package the same volume of cereal. Why then are the boxes shaped as they are?

Companies use rectangular prism boxes to appeal to consumers' brains. The large, flat front and back have more space for colorful graphics. Less eye-catching elements, such as nutritional information, can then be printed on the narrow sides.

No matter what shape your boxes are, remember to always recycle or reuse cardboard when a box is empty.

Math for the Ages

This lab is suitable for all ages. Finding the cube root of the volume may take some help at many levels of education. You can extend this lab from upper elementary on by using different boxes. First write a table of surface area (length multiplied by width for each of the six sides) to the calculated volume. After creating the table, see which type of box is the most cost-effective for cereal companies. Then you can create Cubic Cardboard Boxes for different groups to see the results for multiple sizes.

Right Angle String

Use rope to create a perfect right angle every time.

Geometry Concepts: Right triangles, **surveying**, **Pythagorean theorem**

From the Junk Drawer:

- ☐ String
- ☐ Scissors
- ☐ Ruler
- ☐ Permanent marker
- ☐ 3 pushpins
- ☐ Scrap cardboard
- ☐ Rope (optional)

Step 1: Use your scissors to cut a piece of string 12 inches long. With a ruler and permanent marker, mark inch-long intervals along the entire string.

Step 2: Count three marks in from the end of the string. Push a pushpin through the string to secure it to the piece of scrap cardboard at the third mark. Count 4 inches farther along the string and use another pushpin to hold the next mark in place.

Step 3: Bring the two loose ends of string together and use the third pushpin to secure the ends to the cardboard where they meet. You have just created a perfect right triangle, which has a 90-degree angle. Its sides are 3 inches, 4 inches, and 5 inches long.

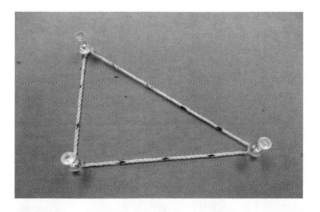

Step 4 (optional): A larger-scale version of this activity can be done with a rope that is 12 feet long. Have students hold the rope at the 3-foot and 7-foot marks. When the loose ends meet to close the triangle, a perfect right angle is formed.

The Math Behind It

Using rope to create perfect right angles is thought to be an ancient Egyptian surveying trick, but scholars have shed doubt on that. Maybe the Egyptians never even used this trick. Regardless of who discovered the method, it works. The Egyptians supposedly used a long rope with 12 equally spaced knots as a measuring tool. Today carpenters still sometimes use this method to check if a corner is a perfect 90 degrees.

The Pythagorean theorem states that the sum of the square of each leg of a right triangle is equal to the square of the **hypotenuse**. So 9 + 16 = 25. Or 3 × 3 + 4 × 4 = 5 × 5. Triangles with sides that are multiples of 3-4-5 length will work.

Math for the Ages

This activity is a great way to introduce the Pythagorean theorem. Older students may even be able to derive the theorem by looking at the numbers 3, 4, and 5.

Soup Can Tangents

Use a soup can to learn what a **tangent** is.

Geometry Concept: Tangent lines to a curve

From the Junk Drawer:

☐ Scissors
☐ Cereal box
☐ Soup can

☐ Paper
☐ Marker

Step 1: Cut the front panel off an empty cereal box. Leave at least one bottom corner fully intact and square.

Step 2: Place the cereal box on a blank piece of paper so the box is upright as it normally would be. Put the can on top of the cereal box base and slide it into the intact corner, as shown. You may need to trim the cardboard so at least one-third of the can extends beyond the bottom of the cereal box. Use your marker to trace around the edge of the can that is exposed to the piece of paper.

Step 3: Trace along both outer edges of the bottom of the cereal box.

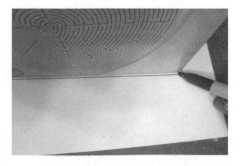

Step 4: Pull the cereal box out from under the can. Match up the bottom of the can with the partial circle you drew in Step 3. Finish tracing around the edge of the can.

Step 5: Remove the can and look at your drawings. The long line and the short line from the cereal box outline represent two tangents to the circle created around the soup can.

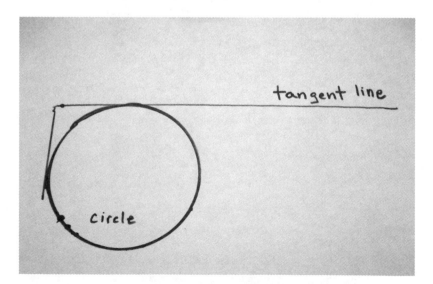

Step 6 (optional): Draw a radius from the center point of the circle to each tangent line. Each radius will be perpendicular to its associated tangent line.

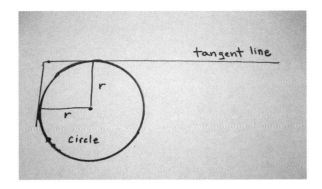

The Math Behind It

Tangents are lines that are perpendicular to a curve at the point where the curve and the line meet. They theoretically only touch the curve at one point, although that is almost impossible to see. Tangents to a circle are perpendicular to the radius of the circle.

Even a shape more complicated than a circle, like a parabola, has a tangent that only touches the curve at one point. This concept will later help students understand calculus.

Math for the Ages

This is a valuable activity to introduce the concept of a tangent line. Different-sized cans work and always gives you the same result. As a group activity, have different people use different-sized cans and then compare their results.

Tangents to curves become important as students reach high school and college. The tangent of a curve is useful to find the slope of a curve at an individual point. The slope will continually change as you move along the curve. The slope of a tangent line to a curve at any point is found by taking the **derivative** of the curve at that point. Derivatives are fundamental to calculus.

Cereal Box Caliper

Create a **caliper** with materials from your recycling bin.

Geometry Concept: Diameter

From the Junk Drawer:

☐ Empty cereal box (or file folders)   ☐ Thumbtack

☐ Scissors   ☐ Brad paper fastener

☐ Marker   ☐ Ruler or tape measure

Step 1: Open an empty cereal box and cut along the edges so the box will lie flat in one big piece. Use your marker to draw a shape that looks similar to a giant number *6* (like the one shown) on the inside of the box. The drawing doesn't have to be precise. Then cut the shape out.

Step 2: Flip the shape over and trace it on another piece of the box. Cut that shape out. When you turn over your original, you should have two identical pieces that are mirror images of each other. Both faces should be blank cardboard, because they are the inside surface of the cereal box.

Step 3: Lay the one piece on top of the other where the bottoms match. Press your thumbtack through the center of both pieces of cardboard and then set the thumbtack aside. Push the brad through the hole you made and then spread the legs of the brad apart on the other side. The cardboard pieces should pivot easily.

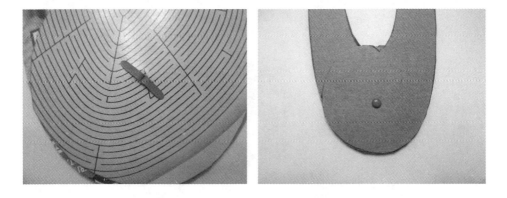

Step 4: Now, calibrate the Cereal Box Caliper so you can use it. Close the top two blades of the caliper until they touch. On the circle part of the caliper, draw a line where the inside edge of the bottom blade intersects the edge of the circle and label this 0. Lay a ruler on the table and open the top blades one inch. Draw another line and label it as 1.

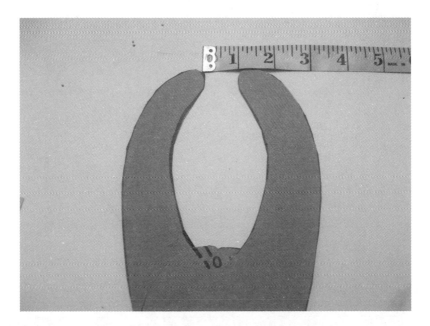

Step 5: Repeat Step 4 to add more inch marks until the calipers are fully open.

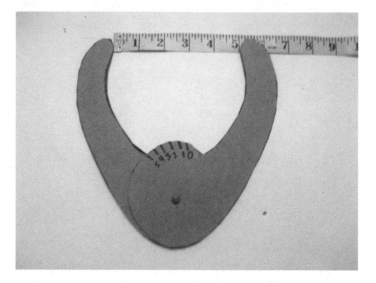

Step 6: Make smaller marks exactly halfway between each inch mark. This allows you to get a more accurate reading with your caliper.

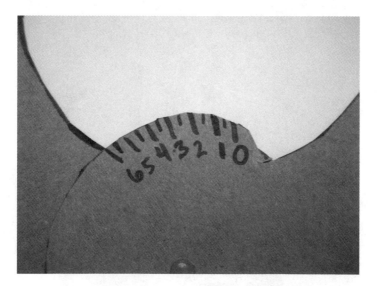

Step 7: Now you are ready to measure. Open your caliper to its widest span. Select a round object, like a can, flagpole, or tree trunk, and bring the tips of the caliper together until they touch the widest part of the object. The

measurement on your caliper represents the diameter of the round object. You should be able to estimate to the nearest half inch.

The Math Behind It

In the real world, measuring the diameter of a solid round object is difficult. It's nearly impossible to stick a ruler through a pipe, pole, or tree. The type of caliper you created is called an outside bow caliper. These are commonly used by arborists (tree scientists). Metal workers also use them to determine the diameter of pipes. Engineers often have calipers close at hand to help them measure tricky round objects. Woodworkers will also use calipers to reproduce table legs when they are making furniture. A different type of caliper, called an inside caliper, measures the inside diameter of pipes and hoses. Calipers are a really cool geometry tool that is used in the everyday world.

Math for the Ages

This activity is suitable for all ages. It is a great way to connect math to the real world, as students often do not see a purpose outside the classroom for what they are learning.

Angle Machine

Determine angles with this simple homemade device.

Geometry Concepts: Determining angles, build a **clinometer**

From the Junk Drawer:

☐ String

☐ Protractor

☐ Tape

☐ Index card

☐ Drinking straw

☐ Scissors

☐ Heavy paper clip or small weight

☐ Marker

Step 1: Attach a string to the middle point of a protractor. If your protractor has a small hole in the center, simply slide the string through this hole and knot the end of the string. If it doesn't have a hole, use a small piece of tape to secure the string at this center point.

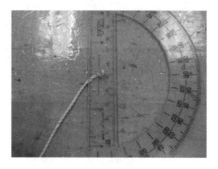

Step 2: Tape a drinking straw to the protractor as shown. Make sure the straw passes over the 0 and 90-degree marks.

Step 3: Tape an index card to the bottom half of the protractor on the opposite side of the straw. One end of the straw should stop at the end of the index card—cut the straw to match the length of the index card if needed. Once turned over, the white of the card makes it easier to read the angle on the protractor.

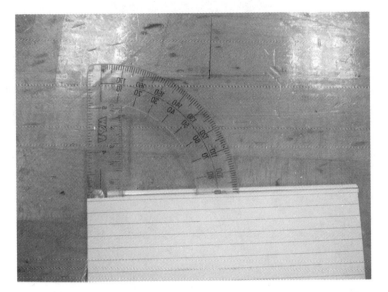

Step 4: Tie a heavy paper clip (or any small weight) to the loose end of the string. The string needs to swing freely as the clinometer moves around.

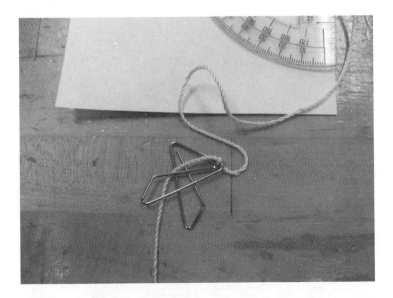

Step 5: Draw an arrow or eyeball on the index card to remind yourself which way to look through the straw. You should be looking down from the free end of the straw, toward the protractor.

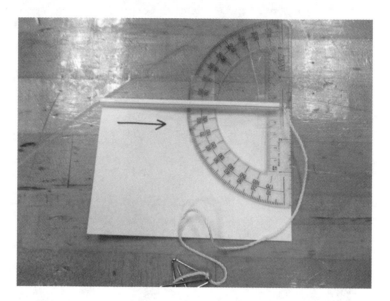

Step 6: Look at the top of a tall object through the end of the straw. Allow the weighted string to hang freely. Without changing the angle of the protractor, check to see where on the protractor the string is hanging. The angle shown (from the zero line) on the protractor tells you the angle from your eye to the top of the tall object.

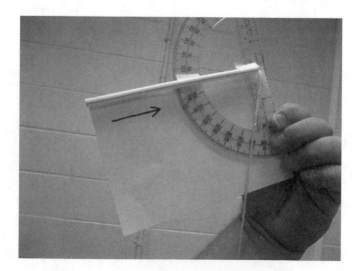

The Math Behind It

Clinometers are used to determine the angles above horizontal. Clinometers were a valuable part of a sextant, a navigational instrument sailors have used for years to locate stars. The angle above horizontal is the same as the lower angle because gravity pulls the paper clip straight down. The string allows the user to measure the angle because the clinometer tilts up from horizontal. The angle above the horizontal is the same as the protractor-string angle is to the zero line.

In addition to sailors, surveying crews also use clinometers. Surveyors are usually seen along major roads wearing bright safety vests and looking through tripods. The tripod contains a more detailed version of a clinometer, and the survey results are used to create road and topographical maps. Model-rocket builders also use clinometers to determine how high their rockets fly.

Math for the Ages

Kids of all ages can use clinometers. Younger children can simply measure the angle between their sightline and tall objects. High school kids can be asked to measure the tangent and solve associated math problems.

Yarn and Cardboard Graph Paper

Make permanent graph paper you can use forever.

Geometry Concepts: Graphing straight lines, slope, and *y*-intercept

From the Junk Drawer:

- ☐ Cardboard
- ☐ Ruler
- ☐ Permanent marker
- ☐ Scissors
- ☐ Pen or pencil
- ☐ Scratch paper
- ☐ Yarn or string

Step 1: Cut a 10-by-10-inch square of cardboard. This activity could be done using cardboard from a recycled cereal box, though you may have to make the graph smaller. If you're in a classroom setting, corrugated cardboard will hold up better. Use a ruler and permanent marker to mark inch-long intervals along each of the four sides.

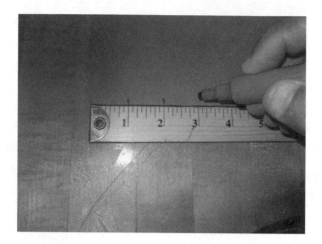

Step 2: Use a ruler and marker to connect the marks on opposing sides of the cardboard, from side-to-side and top-to-bottom. When you're finished, your entire piece of cardboard should be covered in 1-inch squares.

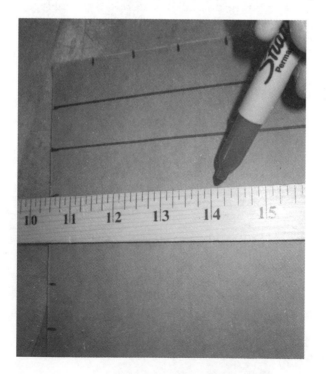

Step 3: Use scissors to cut a small notch at each mark along all edges of the cardboard.

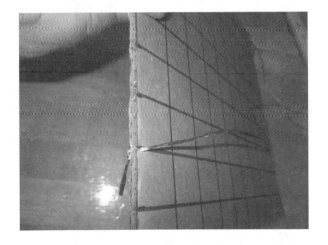

Step 4: Tie a big knot in one end of a piece of yarn or string. Put the knot in one notch.

Step 5: Pull the yarn to the opposite side of the cardboard, loop through another notch, and tie a second knot to secure the yarn in place. You can now calculate the formula for the line. The basic equation for a line is $y = mx + b$—copy this equation onto your scratch paper with your pen or pencil. In this equation, m is the slope of the line (rise divided by run) and b is the y-intercept (the number of marks above zero, or in this case, the number of squares from the edge of the cardboard graph). The *y*-intercept of a line tells you where the line intersects the *y*-axis.

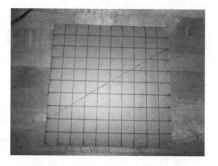

Step 6 (optional): You could also add a second piece of yarn and see where the two pieces of yarn intersect. You could make multiple lines to show the same slope with different y-intercepts.

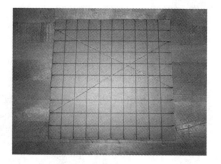

The Math Behind It

Graphing is fundamental to the study of all advanced mathematics. Being able to see and manipulate a graph in a hands-on method aids in comprehension. Straight lines are the best place to start. The function for a straight line ($y = mx + b$) may be the first mathematical function kids learn, but it won't be the last.

Math for the Ages

This activity is suitable for all ages and is an interactive way to introduce the concepts of **slope** and **y-intercept**. Creating two lines and solving for the intersection is a meaningful task for advanced math students.

Unit Circle Glove

Turn an old dishwashing glove into a simple lesson about the coordinates of
the **unit circle**.

Geometry Concepts: Unit circle, hypotenuse, **sine**, **cosine**

From the Junk Drawer:

☐ Disposable dishwashing glove   ☐ Scrap paper
☐ Permanent marker

Step 1: Lay the disposable dishwashing glove down with the palm facing
up. On the tip of the pinky, write *0*. Write *30* on the ring finger, *45* on the
middle finger, *60* on the pointer finger, and *90* on the thumb. In the palm
of the glove, write the symbol for square root ($\sqrt{\ }$) over 2 as a fraction, as
shown. With help from someone else, you can write on the glove while it
is on your hand; this method smooths out the wrinkles in the plastic glove
and makes it easier to write on.

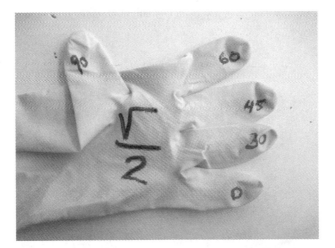

Step 2: If the glove isn't already on your hand, put it on and spread your hand
out so you can see all of the numbers plus the square root on your palm.
Now fold down the finger that you are trying to get the coordinate for.
The number of fingers on either side of the folded finger will tell you the
x- and *y*-coordinates of the unit circle. Simply put the number of fingers

that are still unfolded on the left side of the folded finger under the square root sign. For example, if you fold down the finger that says 30 degrees, you'll still have three unfolded fingers to the left (your middle, pointer, and thumb), so the *x*-coordinate formula is $x = \sqrt{3} \div 2$. Write your equation on a scrap piece of paper so you can reuse the glove.

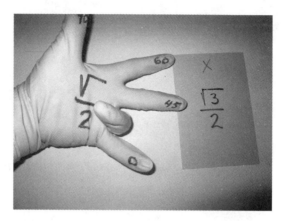

Step 3: Put the number of fingers that remain on the right side of your folder finger under the square root sign. This represents the **y-component** of the unit circle for 30 degrees. Again, write this equation (the square root of right fingers divided by 2) on your scrap paper.

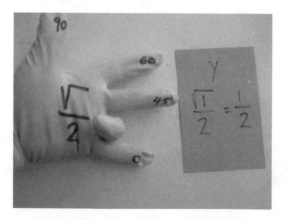

Step 4: It works for all of the angles on your fingertips. For example, bend the 0-degree finger (your pinky). You have four fingers to the left of the bent finger. So the *x*-coordinate is the square root of 4 divided by 2, which equals 1: $\sqrt{4} \div 2 = 2 \div 2 = 1$. You have no fingers to the right of the bent

finger, so the y-coordinate is the square root of 0 divided by 2: $y = \sqrt{0} \div 2 = 0 \div 2 = 0$. So the y-coordinate is 0.

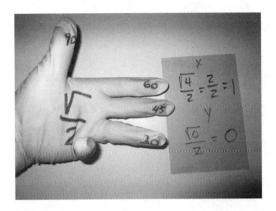

The Math Behind It

A unit circle is a circle with a radius of one. That means that any triangle starting from the center of the circle to the edge of the circle has a hypotenuse of one unit. The sine of an angle is the length of the side opposite the angle divided by the length of the hypotenuse. The cosine of an angle (θ) is the length of the side adjacent to the angle (b) divided by the length of the hypotenuse (c). In each case for the unit circle, you are dividing by 1 ($\cos \theta = b \div c = b \div 1$), so the **adjacent side** (horizontal part) represents the cosine and the opposite side represents the sine of the angle. The angles that most teachers require students to memorize are 0, 30, 45, 60, and 90 degrees. The Unit Circle Glove is a great way to memorize these angles.

Once you know the basic unit circle values, you can simply multiply by the length of the hypotenuse if you have a hypotenuse that is not equal to 1.

Math for the Ages

The unit circle is usually taught in high school, but giving students an earlier glimpse into this concept will give them a great head start. A box of cheap dishwashing gloves would supply a classroom for several years. Most doctors would probably give you a box of medical gloves if you ask, but they are also readily available at many pharmacies. Thicker dishwashing gloves are easier to write on and last longer than exam gloves, but they're also more expensive.

X-Y-Z Box

Use a cardboard box to help visualize **three-dimensional** space.

Geometry Concepts: Three-dimensional coordinate systems

From the Junk Drawer:

☐ Scissors   ☐ Packing tape

☐ Empty cardboard box   ☐ Marker

☐ Meter stick

Step 1: Cut off the top flaps and two sides of a large corrugated cardboard box. You should be left with the bottom flaps and two sides. (You want one corner of the box to stay intact.)

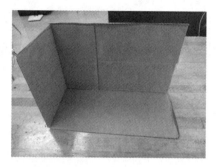

Step 2: One bottom flap bottom will probably be folded inside the box. The X-Y-Z Box looks neater if that flap is outside, since the box's interior will be your workspace. Cut through the tape holding the flaps together, move the inside flap to the outside of the box, and tape it in place with strong packing or duct tape to securely tape.

Step 3: Now you should have three smooth cardboard surfaces. The three-sided box left should be sturdy. Add more tape to strengthen the box if needed.

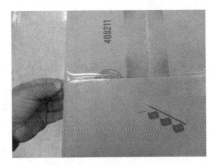

Step 4: Stand the box up facing you so you see a bottom, a left side, and a back, as shown. The back panel represents a normal two-dimensional coordinate system with x- and y-coordinates. The part that sticks out represents the z of a three-dimensional coordinate system. Draw a heavy line along where the bottom and back of the box meet and label that as x. Draw an arrow at the end of the line to indicate that it will go on forever.

Step 5: Draw a dark line along where the back and side meet and label that as y. This line will also go on forever, so add the arrow here too.

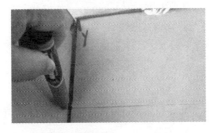

Step 6: Draw a third dark line along where the bottom and side meet, and label that as z. End your line with an arrow.

Step 7: Draw grid lines on all three interior **planes**, using the width of a meter stick. Butt the meter stick into one corner and then trace along the edge. Then line it up with the line you just drew and draw a line on the other side of the stick. Repeat until most of the panel is covered.

Step 8: Turn the meter stick perpendicular the first set of lines and draw the next set of grid lines. Repeat until all panels are covered in the grid.

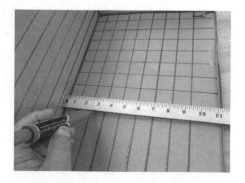

Step 9: Your finished X-Y-Z Box should look like this.

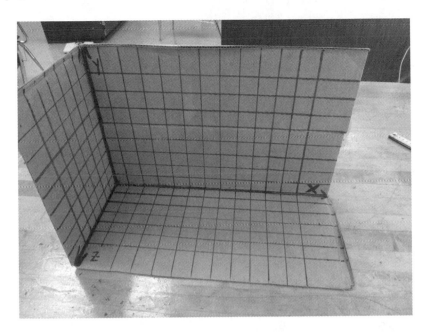

Step 10 (optional): You can store your X-Y-Z Box by putting it on your bookshelf and putting books in it. This will keep the box square when you are not using it and prevent it from being crushed.

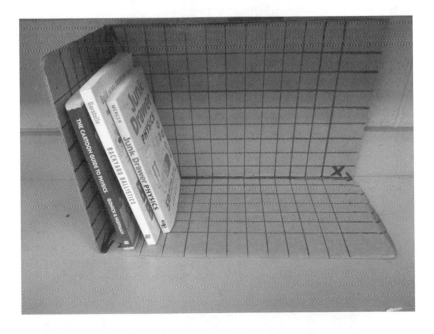

The Math Behind It

Space is three-dimensional. Students typically grow comfortable with two dimensions quickly, because that can easily be seen on graph paper. Three-dimensional spaces can be hard to visualize, but the X-Y-Z Box makes the concept easier to envision. Although the box only represents one **quadrant** of three-dimensional space, it is easier to see where a negative z-point would be than it is on graph paper. Three-dimensional coordinates are usually written in parentheses as (*2, 3, 4*). The *2* represents the x-part. The *3* represents the y-part. And the *4* represents the z-part. So this point would be 2 spaces over, 3 spaces up, and 4 spaces out.

Math for the Ages

Students usually encounter three-dimensional space in high school, but the concept is easily understood at lower levels of school. Giving young students an early look at three-dimensional space is beneficial. This could be done in a smaller group setting using shoeboxes for an in-class activity. One math teacher in my school uses the corner of his classroom to teach three-dimensional space because the school's walls are cinderblock and the spaces between the blocks can represent the grid lines.

2

Geometry Labs

Math is best learned by doing. And there is no better way to do math than math labs. Seeing, touching, and feeling math concepts will give students a better sense of the concepts. When students connect real-world applications to math concepts from school, they internalize the concepts.

So, let's get our hands dirty and do some geometry.

A Voyage with Vectors

Use straws to learn the key to how airplanes fly.

Geometry Concepts: **Vector** addition, **resultants**

From the Junk Drawer:

☐ Scissors
☐ Colored construction paper
☐ Tape
☐ Drinking straws of various lengths

☐ Dry-erase marker
☐ Whiteboard (or poster board)
☐ Ruler

Step 1: Cut three or four small, narrow triangles out of colored construction paper. They can be any colors or sizes. Tape the triangles to the ends of three or four drinking straws of different lengths. The straws can be randomly cut. Draw a simple two-dimensional (x-y) graph on the

51

whiteboard with a dry-erase marker. If you don't have a whiteboard, a piece of poster board will work just as well. Place one of the straws with the tail (nontriangle end) at the origin of the *x-y* plane. This straw represents a vector. Label this first vector *vector A*. The common way of denoting that the **line segment** is a vector is to draw a small arrow over the *A*.

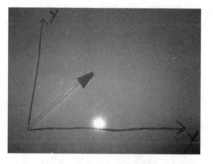

Step 2: The key to adding straw vectors is to use the "tip-to-tail" method. Place the tail of the second vector at the tip (triangle end) of the first vector. Label the second straw *Vector B*. The straws don't have to be in a perfectly straight line.

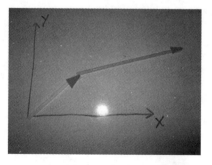

Step 3: With a long ruler, draw a straight line from the origin to the arrow of the second vector.

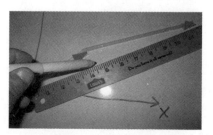

Step 4: Draw an arrow at the ending point of the second vector. This line represents the sum of Vector A and Vector B. This sum is called a resultant for vector addition.

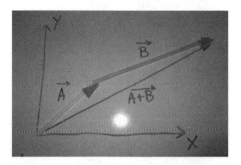

Step 5: To add three (or more) vectors, just follow the same procedure from the previous steps. If you used a whiteboard, erase $A + B$ to calculate new vectors. If you are using a piece of paper, move to a clean area on the paper. Now place another vector C at the end of vector B. Again, your new vector can be tilted in any forward direction.

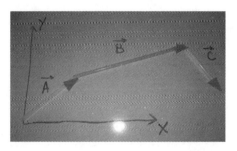

Step 6: Draw a straight line from your origin to the triangle at the end of Vector C. This line represents the sum of $A + B + C$. This sum is also called a resultant for vector addition.

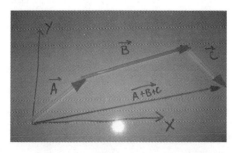

The Math Behind It

Vectors are directed line segments. Vectors can be used to represent **displacements**, velocities, and forces. The length is related to value of the vector. The direction of the line segment represents the direction that the vector is pointing in. In using the tip-to-tail method of vector addition, you never change the length or the direction as you add them. The sum of all the vectors you add is a straight line from the starting point to the end point. This line is called the resultant.

Vectors are taught in math classes and classes for engineering, physics, and navigation. When flying an airplane, pilots fly legs of a flight. To stay safe, they don't fly in a straight line from their starting city to their finishing city. Air traffic controllers tell them the legs that they must fly, in order to keep planes spaced far apart for safety. The legs are almost like lanes on a busy road. If you add all of the individual legs, you will get the resultant of a trip. The resultant is a straight line from the starting to the finish point. Knowing how to add vectors is a skill that will aid in your pursuit of a STEM career.

Math for the Ages

Vectors are traditionally taught in high school courses, but there is no reason kids can't learn about vectors earlier. Teaching with colored straws or pipe cleaners helps students understand the concept better; anytime you can add a visual component to a concept, it will help kids' comprehension.

Area and Perimeter Flooring

Use painter's tape and a tile floor to learn about area and **perimeter**.

Geometry Concepts: Area and perimeter

From the Junk Drawer:

- ☐ Painter's tape
- ☐ Square-tile floor
- ☐ Ruler or yardstick

Step 1: Use painter's tape to create different outlines on a tile floor. Make sure your shape is exclusively made of right angles. Press down on the painter's tape very lightly so you can easily pull it up and reposition it. Square floor tiles are ideal for this activity, since the tiles are uniform in size—usually one square foot.

Step 2: Calculate the perimeter by measuring the outside edge of each shape with a ruler. If the flooring is made up of square-foot tiles, simply count the foot-long segments.

Step 3: Calculate the area of each shape by dividing it into simple areas—for example, two rectangles. You can use painter's tape or meter sticks to help you see how to divide up the area. Add the small areas together to get the total area. In a classroom setting, let small groups of students create their own shapes and calculate the area. When they're done calculating the area of their group's shape, they can calculate the area of other students' shapes.

Step 4 (optional): Depending on the knowledge level of students, you can add angled lines to the shapes. You still need to divide the area into simple areas to calculate the total area. Angled lines necessitate including triangles in your calculations. The formula for the area of a triangle is 0.5 × base × height.

The Math Behind It

Area is not a simple calculation if the area is an odd shape. Calculating areas of oddball shapes is a valuable skill to learn for upper-level math, physics, and engineering students. Area under a curve is found by using calculus. In calculus, to solve, you divide the curved area into small rectangles using a method called integration. Students who understand that a complicated area is solved by splitting the area into simpler areas will have a leg up as math gets harder.

Perimeter is best understood as fencing around a yard or pasture. Perimeter is simply the length of the fence required to enclose any area.

Math for the Ages

This is a great, fun lab to teach area and perimeter. Students of almost any age could do this. Young children would be fine with squares and rectangles only. Elementary-age students would probably do OK with shapes that are combinations of rectangles. Middle school students could handle angled lines, meaning you will need to include triangles in addition to rectangles. With great care and patience, you could even create curves for high school kids, but you would need to approximate the shape with rectangles and triangles. Calculating the areas of curves using small rectangles is one of the main components of calculus, so this would be a novel way to introduce the concept to teenagers.

Pipe Cleaner Translations

Use pipe cleaners to learn about **translation** of functions.

Geometry Concepts: Translations of functions, $y = mx + b$

From the Junk Drawer:

☐ Graph paper   ☐ Pipe cleaners

☐ Pen or pencil

Step 1: Draw an x-axis and a y-axis in the center of your graph paper using the grid lines as a guide. Then have students straighten a pipe cleaner into a straight line. Lay it diagonally on a sheet of graph paper so it intersects the center of your graph. Then write the equation $y = mx + b$ in the margin of the paper. The m in the equation represents the slope (rise divided by run). The b represents where the line crosses the y-axis. For our line, that is zero. So your equation would be $y = mx + 0$.

Step 2: Move the pipe cleaner up two units on the y-axis. Write the new equation, taking into account the new y-axis position. Remember that when a graph is translated, it is only slid; you do not change anything else about the graph. So the new equation would be $y = mx + 2$.

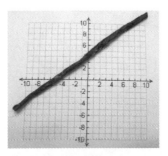

Step 3: Depending on the student's level, you can bend the pipe cleaner into a parabola, a sine curve, and so on. Once you create a function, you can translate it up or down and side to side. The important thing to realize in a translation is that you only shift the function; nothing else changes.

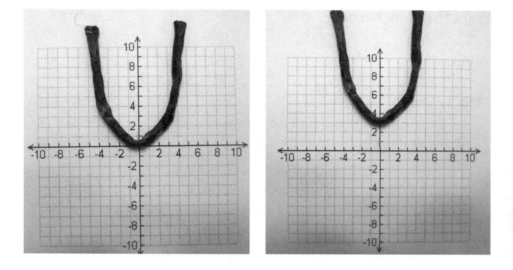

The Math Behind It

A *translation* is a term used in geometry to describe a function that is moved a certain distance—nothing else about the function changes. The function is not rotated or resized. You are basically just sliding the function up or down a set distance. Translation is also a term used in physics, so seeing the same topic in different subjects really helps students understand it better and recognize its many applications.

Math for the Ages

This activity is a simple, visual way to introduce the y-intercept in the $y = mx + b$ equation. For higher-level students, the functions get more complicated, but it is still just sliding the function a set distance.

Cheese Cracker Pythagoras

Here's an edible way to reinforce Pythagoras's famous theorem.

Geometry Concept: Pythagorean theorem

From the Junk Drawer:

☐ Square cheese crackers (or small   ☐ Small square object
square cereal)

Step 1: Lay four cheese cracker squares in a straight line. Place a small square object against the line of crackers.

Step 2: Lay three cheese cracker squares along the other side of the square object, so they are perpendicular to your first line of crackers. Remove the square object you used to help you create the perfect 90-degree angle between your two lines of crackers.

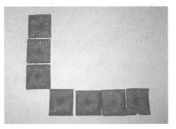

Step 3: Lay five cheese cracker squares to form a hypotenuse and complete the triangle.

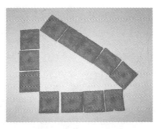

Step 4: On the triangle legs with three squares, make a 3-by-3 square using cheese crackers.

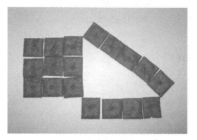

Step 5: Repeat for the other two sides with a 4-by-4-inch square of crackers on the other leg, and a 5-by-5-inch square of crackers along the hypotenuse. Now you have the Pythagorean Theorem ($a^2 + b^2 = c^2$) made out of cheese crackers! You can prove the theorem by adding up the crackers from both legs—they should be equal to the number of crackers along the hypotenuse.

The Math Behind It

Pythagoras's famous theorem ($a^2 + b^2 = c^2$) was probably known before he was ever alive. He (or his followers) is considered to be the first to provide written proof that the theorem works. The hypotenuse squared (c^2) is equal to the sum of the individual other sides squared ($a^2 + b^2$). This formula is exceptionally important when using right triangles.

Math for the Ages

This activity works best after the Pythagorean theorem is introduced in late elementary school. Even before the theorem is introduced, it is a fun activity for younger children to do at home to give them an advanced look at the topic.

This activity is a hands-on method of internalizing the theorem. Advanced students could try different-length right-angle sides, but the hypotenuse may not always be a perfect square. A great way to start is with 3-4-5 triangles.

Inscribed Angle Circles

Learn the **inscribed angle** theorems with rubber bands.

Geometry Concepts: Inscribed angle theorems

From the Junk Drawer:

☐ Paper

☐ Large piece of corrugated cardboard or foam core board

☐ Small plate or round, flat object

☐ Marker

☐ Rubber bands

☐ Thumbtacks or pushpins

☐ Protractor

☐ Ruler (optional)

Step 1: Turn over a small plate or any round, flat object and trace a circle around it onto the paper. You could also use the compass you created from this book to draw a perfect circle.

Step 2: Find the center of the circle by holding the paper up to a bright light. You will be able to see the lines of the circle through the paper. Bring the sides of the paper together until the two sides of the circle perfectly overlap and you only see a **semicircle**. Crease the bend in the paper with your fingernail to make the halfway point. You don't have to crease the entire width, but you want to crease most of it. Unfold the paper.

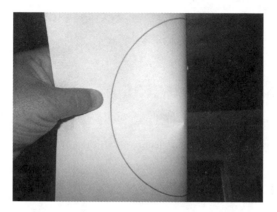

Step 3: Fold the semicircle in half the opposite way. While holding the paper up to a bright light, line up the two sides of the semicircle through the semitranslucent paper and crease the point. The point where the two creased lines intersect will be the center of your circle.

Step 4: Unfold the paper and lay it circle side up on top of the corrugated cardboard or foam core board. Use a marker to label C for the center of the circle and darken in the center point.

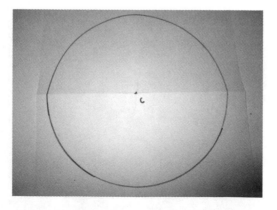

Step 5: Place two rubber bands directly over the center point, and then press a thumbtack or pushpin into point C so the pin goes through the rubber bands, the paper, and the cardboard.

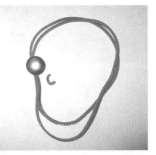

Step 6: Place two pushpins on opposing sides of the bottom of the circle. Stretch one central rubber band over each of the bottom pushpins. Put the rubber bands on the bottom metal part of the pushpin so that the two sides of the rubber band touch, forming almost a perfect line (rather than two parallel lines).

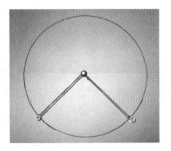

Step 7: Put another pushpin somewhere at the top of the circle on the circle's **circumference**. Stretch a rubber band from each of the bottom pins to the top pin.

Step 8: Measure the top angle with a protractor. This angle is called an inscribed angle. An inscribed angle is any angle that is created by three points on the circumference of a circle.

Step 9: Measure the **central angle**. The central angle of a circle is any angle formed by the center of the circle and two radii. The central angle should be twice the inscribed angle above. At this point you could remove the rubber bands and pushpins and, using a ruler, connect all the pushpin holes to create a page for your notebook or really cool wall art.

Step 10: An interesting use of this theorem is to discover what happens when the pushpins are placed at the diameter of the circle. The central angle at that point would be the entire bottom of the circle, which is 180 degrees. Place two pushpins on the diameter you folded at the beginning. Place

another pushpin somewhere on the top semicircle circumference. Trap two rubber bands under the pushpin.

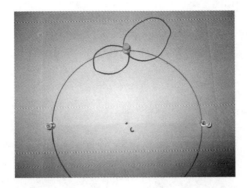

Step 11: Connect all of the pins with rubber bands. What do you notice about the triangle?

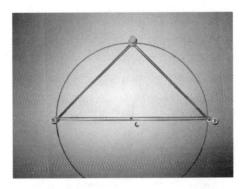

Step 12: Use a protractor to measure the top inscribed angle. It will be 90 degrees; the triangle is a right triangle.

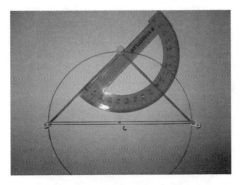

Step 13: Now move the top pushpin to any point on the top semicircle circumference and check the new inscribed angle with your protractor. This arrangement of pushpins will always result in a right triangle.

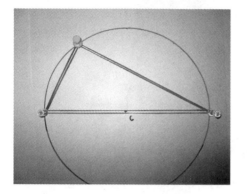 

The Math Behind It

Circles are beautiful. The geometry of circles is also beautiful. The circle theorems deal with angles and **chords** inside the circle. One of the most important circle theorems is the **central angle theorem**, which says that any inscribed angle will be twice the central angle. It can be proved mathematically on paper, which might be a great thing to do if you draw all of the rubber band lines.

An interesting part of the central angle theorem is that any angle inscribed in a semicircle will be a right triangle. A semicircle is made when the bottom is a diameter. For a diameter, the central angle is equal to 180 degrees. By the central angle theorem, the inscribed angle must be 90 degrees.

Math for the Ages

Circle theorems are taught at the high school level, but younger students can easily understand them. Front-loading their brains before high school will lead to greater math success. Using a semicircle is a great way for even the youngest students to understand the terms *diameter*, *semicircle*, *right triangle*, and *inscribed angle*. As always, remember that early success in math leads to continued success in math.

Linear, Area, and Volume Markers

Use old file folders to learn the difference between **linear**, area, and volume measurement.

Geometry Concepts: Linear, area, and volume units

From the Junk Drawer:

- ☐ Old file folders, cereal boxes, or heavy construction paper
- ☐ Scissors
- ☐ Ruler
- ☐ Marker
- ☐ Tape

Step 1: Cut a strip from an old file folder that is ¼ inch wide and 1 inch long. Label it *1 inch*. (Note: this entire activity could be done with centimeters if you can write really small.)

Step 2: Cut a 1-by-1-inch square from the file folder. Label this *1 square inch*, *1 sq. in.*, or *1 in²*.

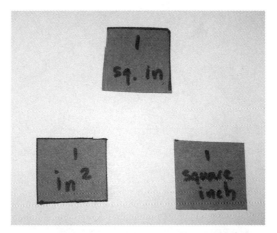

Step 3: Making a cube is a little tougher. Trace the square inch from Step 2 to start. Then trace five more squares to make the shape of a *T*, as shown. Write *1 cubic inch* (or *1 cu. in.* or *1 in³*) on each side of the square.

Step 4: Cut out the *T* and bend each line into a 90-degree angle.

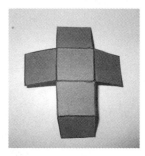

Step 5: Fold four sides up and use a small piece of tape to hold the cube together. Finally, fold the top over to create the cube.

Step 6: Now, look at various things around you and decide which marker would be the best for measuring. What if you were measuring the area of a piece of paper? The square inch works best. The length of your pencil? The ¼-by-1-inch strip works best. The volume of a mac and cheese box? The cubic inch.

The Math Behind It

Inches, square inches, and cubic inches have different meanings but can be confusing as you first learn about them. Inches are used to measure linear distances (one dimension), like the length of your index finger. Square inches are used to measure the area of flat shapes (two dimensions), like a piece of paper. Cubic inches are used to measure the volume of three-dimensional shapes, like a cereal box.

Linear, square, and cubic units can be found for almost all of the common units. Kilometers, square kilometers, and cubic kilometers would be perfect units if you needed to measure something really big like a soccer field and stadium. Centimeters, square centimeters, and cubic centimeters, would be good for measuring something smaller, like a textbook.

Many things you buy are sold in linear units. Ribbon, string, and electrical wires are all sold based on their linear feet (or meters). Square units are used for materials that have to cover areas. Wrapping paper, floor tile, and carpeting are all sold in square units. Cubic units are used to measure volumes of materials. Concrete is sold in cubic yards, and concrete trucks generally hold 5 to 7 cubic yards of concrete. Cubic centimeters are commonly used to measure small engines for machines like go-karts and motorcycles. For a 250cc motorcycle, the *cc* stands for the cubic centimeters inside the engine. The bigger the volume, the faster the motorcycle could go. Cubic centimeters are also commonly used in the medical field for measuring medicines.

Math for the Ages

This activity is suitable for all ages. It even can be done by high school students so they understand the difference between the three types of basic measurement units. A great lab for most ages is to measure a book. Ask the students to measure the length of each side, the area of a single page, and the volume of the book. Having their linear, area, and volume markers handy will help them understand the concept better.

Marshmallow Volume

Build rectangular solids to learn about volume.

Geometry Concept: Volume versus side length

From the Junk Drawer:

☐ 64 mini-marshmallows   ☐ Glue (optional)

☐ Toothpicks (optional)

Step 1: Lay the marshmallows on your work area in a square, using 2 marshmallows on each side. How many marshmallows make up the square?

Step 2: Build a cube of marshmallows that is 2 marshmallows high, 2 marshmallows long, and 2 marshmallows wide by adding to your original square What is the volume of the cube, in terms of marshmallows? The number of marshmallows represents the volume of the shape.

Step 3: Add another row of marshmallows to one end. You now have a rectangular solid, sometimes called a rectangular prism. What is the volume of marshmallows now?

Step 4: Now create a cube that is 3 marshmallows high, 3 long, and 3 wide. You might want to spear the marshmallows on toothpicks to hold them in place. You could also glue them together if you want, but you can't eat them afterward then. Stacking the marshmallows is fun but challenging.

Step 5: Add another 3-by-3 square of marshmallows to one end of your marshmallow cube. What is the volume now? Can you come up with the formula to solve for volume of a rectangular solid, like your marshmallow rectangle?

The Math Behind It

Volume is the three-dimensional space an object occupies. It depends upon length, width, and height. For a rectangular solid, you simply multiply those three dimensions to find the volume: $V = l \times w \times h$.

Math for the Ages

This activity is best suited for young students. By upper elementary, students have already been taught that volume (V) equals length (l) times width (w) times height (h) for a rectangular solid. This is a fun way to review $V = l \times w \times h$ and give the students a little marshmallow treat once they're done building their shapes.

Midsegment Toilet Paper

Learn the **midsegment theorem** using a piece of toilet paper.

Geometry Concept: Midsegment theorem

Junk Drawer Material:

- ☐ Square of toilet paper (or any thin paper)
- ☐ Marker
- ☐ Ruler

Step 1: Use a marker to draw a triangle on a square of toilet paper or any thin piece of paper. Label the **vertices** A, B, and C.

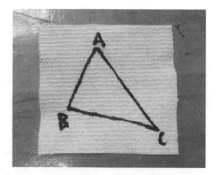

Step 2: Fold the piece of paper over so two vertices line up. Thin paper, like toilet paper, allows you to easily see the vertices that you are lining up. Slightly pinch the paper on the fold.

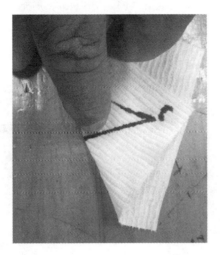

Step 3: Unfold it and draw a large dot on the pinch point. This dot represents the midpoint of that side of the triangle.

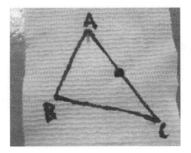

Step 4: Repeat Steps 2 and 3 for another side of the triangle. Label the midpoint with another large dot.

Step 5: Connect the two large dots with your ruler and draw a line between them. This vertical line represents the midpoint of the triangle. Measure the base (the side parallel to the midsegment) of the triangle. Also measure the length of the midsegment. What do you notice about the lengths?

Step 6: You can repeat the above steps for the other two sides of the triangle and further verify the midsegment theorem.

The Math Behind It

The midsegment theorem states that the **segment** joining the midpoints of two sides of a triangle with be parallel to the third side and half of its length. The midsegment theorem also helps understand **similar triangles**. The large and the small triangles you created are similar since they have the same angle measurements.

Math for the Ages

The midsegment theorem is usually taught in high school geometry. This activity lets high schoolers see a visual representation of the thereom. And the creative use of an unusual material (toilet paper) will help students remember the lesson. You can also introduce segments, midpoints, and parallel lines to even the youngest children with this quick activity.

Parallel Paper Plate Proof

Deduce the area of a circle using an inexpensive paper plate.

Geometry Concepts: Area and radius of a circle

From the Junk Drawer:

☐ Thin paper plate   ☐ Scissors

☐ Marker   ☐ Ruler

☐ Crayons (optional)

Step 1: Fold a paper plate in half and crease the fold with your fingers.

Step 2: Fold the halved paper plate again and crease the folded edge.

Step 3: Fold the quarter paper plate again and crease the folded edge.

Step 4: Unfold the paper plate. Use a ruler and a marker to trace all of the fold lines. You should have eight **sections**.

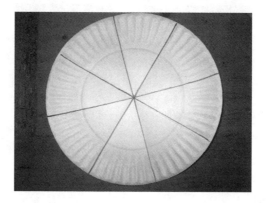

Step 5: Use crayons or a marker to color in four of the eight sections that make up the paper plate.

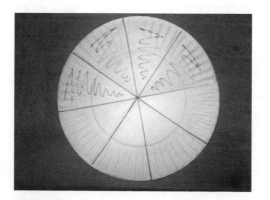

Step 6: Cut all eight sections apart with scissors. Create a parallelogram by alternating the directions and colors of the wedges, as shown.

Step 7: The formula for the area of the parallelogram is found by multiplying base times height ($A = b \times h$). The base is made of the four bottom wedges that are the same color. The base is made up of half of the circle, which is half of the circle's circumference. Measure the height of the parallelogram with your ruler. The height of the parallelogram is the radius of the paper plate.

Step 8: Now you can calculate the area using the radius you just measured. Area is equal to the base times height. Area is equal to pi (π) times the radius (r) squared: $A = \pi \times r^2$

$$A = b \times h$$
$$b = \tfrac{1}{2}C = \tfrac{1}{2}(2\pi r) = \pi r$$
$$h = r$$
$$\text{So } A = \pi \times r \times r = \pi r^2$$

The Math Behind It

$A = \pi \times r^2$ is one of the most useful area formulas. Virtually every adult remembers this formula from school. This activity is a great way to internalize the true meaning of this formula.

Math for the Ages

This activity is suitable for almost all grade levels above preschool, and kids can do this individually or in pairs. It is also a great way to introduce proofs in geometry. A proof is when you use what you know to prove something you may or may not know. A package of cheap paper plates keeps the cost extremely low.

Radians Are Fun

Yarn and scissors teach students what a **radian** is.
Geometry Concept: Radians

From the Junk Drawer:

- ☐ Yarn (or string)
- ☐ Ruler
- ☐ Scissors
- ☐ Calculator
- ☐ Pen or pencil
- ☐ Scrap paper

Step 1: Cut two 100-centimeter pieces of yarn or string. Using two different colors of yarn may help you visualize the concept better. Then, using a calculator, divide 100 by 6.28 (6.28 = $\pi \times 2$) and write the answer down on a piece of scrap paper.

Step 2: Cut one of the 100-centimeter pieces of yarn into centimeter lengths equal to the calculator value you just wrote down. You will end up with six full lengths and a small, partial piece left over.

Step 3: Lay the uncut 100-centimeter piece of yarn on a table and form it into the best circle possible.

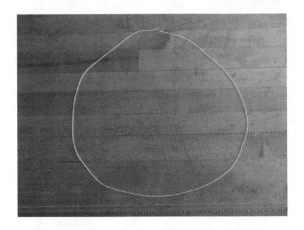

Step 4: Lay the six cut pieces of yarn on top of the circle you just created.

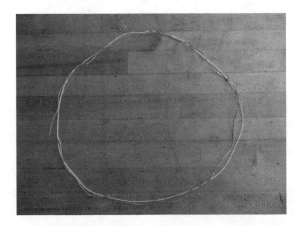

Step 5: Repeat Steps 1 and 2, but use 60 centimeters of yarn instead of 100. Place the uncut 60-centimeter piece inside the larger circle. Form the 60-centimeter length into a circle. Move the 60-centimeter circle until the 100-centimeter circle and 60-centimeter circle look as if they have the same center. Place the six cut 60-centimeter pieces on top of the 60-centimeter circle. You should now have two circles, each with two layers of yarn.

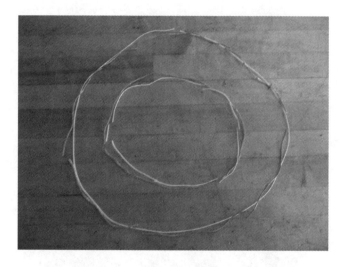

Step 6: Take a cut piece from the 60-centimeter circle and point it toward the center of the circle. The section pointing inward is the same size as the radius of the smaller circle.

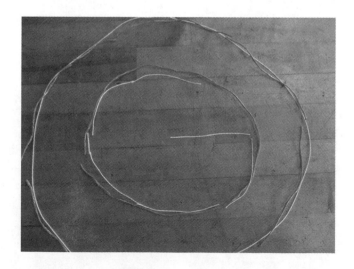

Step 7: Repeat for the larger, 100-centimeter circle. The cut piece is also the same size as the radius of the larger circle.

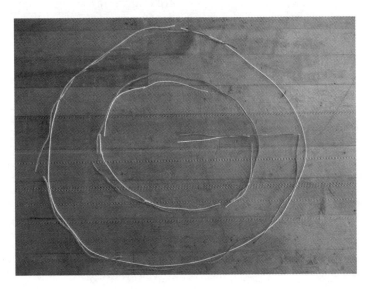

Step 8: Cut two longer pieces of yarn. Place one of the longer pieces of yarn from the center out past the edge of the largest circle. Move the cut pieces of both circles until they line up with the longer yarn. Place the other longer piece of yarn at the other end of the cut piece as shown. The angle between the two longer yarn pieces is called a radian. Notice how one radian is the same for both of the circles.

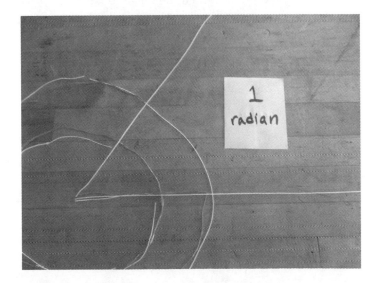

The Math Behind It

Every circle has 6.28 radii around it. The **arc** length of the equivalent length of one radius on the outside edge of the circle is called a radian. A smaller circle will have a smaller radius, but the smaller circle still has 6.28 radians around its circumference. Where does the number 6.28 come from? Well, 6.28 = 2 × π (π = 3.14). One half-circle would be equal to pi.

Angles can be measured in either radians or degrees. Mathematicians, for example, often measure angles in radians. Scientific calculators will do calculations in both degrees and radians. If you want to switch between degrees and radians on a scientific calendar, press the button that says *mode* or *DRG*.

Math for the Ages

Radians are generally not taught until middle school, but younger students can understand the concept. This can also be related to the circumference equation: $C = 2 \times \pi \times r$.

Allow middle school and high school students to call it radiuses at first. Language art teachers may object, but students usually understand it better. They will shift to calling it a radian quickly enough.

This activity is a must for high school students. Even if they have encountered the concept before, the activity will reinforce what they learned. My physics students do this at every level to help them understand radians. Most classrooms will also have students who have never before seen this concept firsthand.

Smartphone Trig

Use a free smartphone app to help kids learn **trigonometry**.

Geometry Concepts: Right-triangle trigonometry, adjacent side, **opposite side**

From the Junk Drawer:

☐ Smartphone with clinometer app
☐ Several books
☐ Board
☐ 2 meter sticks or rulers

☐ Scratch paper
☐ Pen or pencil
☐ Scientific calculator

Step 1: Search your smartphone's app store for a free clinometer (also referred to as an angle meter or a bubble level) app. Download the clinometer app on your smartphone.

Step 2: Stack several books on a table with their spines aligned and lean a board on top of the books to create an incline. To create a right triangle on a level surface, place one meter stick flat on the table and hold another meter stick vertically against the inclined board, as shown. The meter sticks represent the legs of the triangle, and the board represents the hypotenuse. Open the app on your smartphone and place the phone on the board. Most clinometer apps will read an angle from both vertical and horizontal. You want to use the angle from horizontal, which should be between 0 and 45 degrees.

Step 3: Look at the meter stick that forms the base of the triangle. In trigonometry, this base is also called the adjacent side of the triangle. Use the other meter stick to measure the height of the triangle at a base length of your choosing. Repeat at several base distances: 10 centimeters, 20 centimeters, 30 centimeters, and so on. (You can also measure in inches if you'd prefer.) The standing meter stick that you used to measure the base distances represents the height of the triangle. In trigonometry, this is also called the opposite side, because it is opposite of the angle.

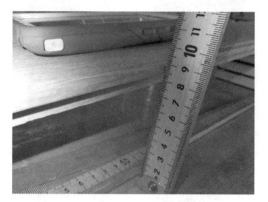

Step 4: Write a table of opposite side lengths and adjacent side lengths on a piece of scrap paper. Use a scientific calculator to divide the opposite side by the adjacent side for each set of values. What do you see about the ratios for each set of values?

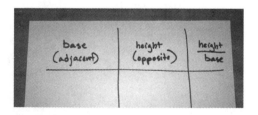

The Math Behind It

Trigonometry—the study of angles—is one of the earliest areas of mathematics created. Right-triangle trigonometry is one of engineers', surveyors', and construction contractors' most useful tools.

By measuring a triangle's height and angle or length along the ground and the angle, you can determine everything about the triangle. The opposite side (height) divided by the adjacent side (length) is the tangent of the angle (tangent of angle = $h \div l$). The ratio of height over length for a right triangle is always the same, no matter the base length. You can check your value with a scientific calculator. When you put the average of all the ratios into a scientific calculator and press the *tan-1* button, the angle measurement should be very close to the value the clinometer app showed.

Math for the Ages

Trigonometry is a high school course, but this lab can really be done with all ages. The youngest children will gain an understanding of angles at an early age. They may just get to enjoy watching the angle change as they move the phone around.

This lab would be a great way to teach upper-elementary and middle school students about angles, ratios, and right triangles, even if they don't actually calculate the tangent of the angle.

For high school math students, this lab is a must. It is a great way to introduce right-triangle trigonometry. Let the students discover that the ratios of the sides are equal before you explain sine, cosine, and tangent. A fun option is to create a table that also includes the hypotenuse at each base measurement. The students could then verify that sine is equal to the opposite (height) divided by the hypotenuse ($\sin \theta$ = opposite $\div$ hypotenuse), and the cosine is equal to the adjacent (base) divided by the hypotenuse ($\cos \theta$ = adjacent $\div$ hypotenuse).

Straw Components

Find the secret to vector components using drinking straws.

Geometry Concepts: Right-triangle components, vectors

From the Junk Drawer:

☐ Paper

☐ Pen or pencil

☐ Drinking straws

☐ Scissors

Step 1: Draw an x-y set of axes on a piece of paper. Place a drinking straw at an angle with one end at the origin.

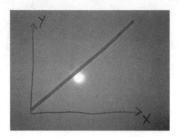

Step 2: Stand another straw up at the end of the first straw. The second straw should be perpendicular to the x-axis. Cut the second straw so that the end is at the tip of the first straw. The second straw represents the y-component of the first vector. The y-component is the part of the vector that points in the same direction as the y-axis.

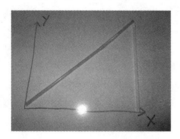

Step 3: Lay a third straw along the x-axis, perpendicular to the y-axis. Cut the third straw so that it fits between the first two straws. This third straw represents the **x-component** of the first vector. The x-component is the part of the vector that points in the same direction as the x-axis. The right triangle you have assembled out of straws shows you the x- and the y-components of the first vector.

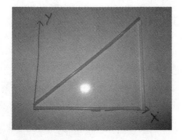

Step 4: Repeat Steps 1–3 for the same vector of a different angle. Notice how the x- and y-components are now different lengths.

The Math Behind It

Vectors are crucial to math, physics, and engineering. All vectors can be split into an x-component and a y-component. If you use vectors, you can get your initial vector by adding the x- and y-components. Vectors can be used to represent forces, displacements, velocities, and accelerations. Separating vectors into the x-part and y-part will help you understand them and begin on the path to solving difficult problems.

Math for the Ages

Vectors are traditionally taught in high school, but younger students can grasp the concept of components. This would give them a head start when they see it later. Adding a hands-on component gives older students a visual component that helps most students better understand the concept. There are a couple of ways to add to this lab. First, you can use it to verify the Pythagorean theorem. Measure each of the components. If you then square each component and add them, you should get the length of the main vector squared ($a^2 + b^2 = c^2$). Second, you can verify sine and cosine if your students are already familiar with those concepts. Measure the angle with a protractor and the length of the main vector with a ruler. The main vector length multiplied by the cosine of the angle should equal the length of the x-component. The main vector length multiplied by the sine of the angle should equal the length of the y-component. You can also make the first arrow small enough that it will fit on notebook paper. Then the students can have a visual study aid at home. Adding color, visual aids, and hands-on learning will help students get math.

Straw Triangles

Cut drinking straws to learn the different kinds of triangles.

Geometry Concepts: Different types of triangles

From the Junk Drawer:

☐ 3 paper clips   ☐ Scissors

☐ 3 drinking straws   ☐ Protractor (optional)

Step 1: Using both hands, unbend a paper clip at the center until the two overlapping ends separate, as shown. Unbend at least three paper clips.

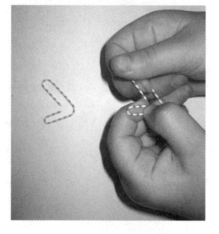

Step 2: Pick up one of your unbent paper clips and slide a straw on either end of it. (If you want to save plastic, you can cut one straw in half and place one piece on either end of the paper clip.) The straws should form a *v* shape held together by the paper clip.

Step 3: Slide unbent paper clips into the other ends of both straws already suspended on a paper clip. Slide the third straw onto the exposed end of each paper clip. You have created an equilateral triangle, which has three equal sides.

Step 4: Remove one straw from the triangle and cut it in half. After cutting, put one piece back to form the third side again. You will need to bend the other paper clip a little closer together. You can probably leave the straws on the paper clip as you bend it. You have now created an isosceles triangle with two equal sides and two equal angles.

Step 5: Remove both of the longer straws. Cut them to different lengths than the remaining straw that you already cut. You want three different-length pieces. Bend the clips as needed to slide the straws back on the three paper clips to complete a new triangle. This is called a scalene triangle, which has three unequal sides.

Step 6: With scissors and bending the clips, you can create the three different types of scalene triangles: acute, right, and obtuse. An acute triangle has three angles that are less than 90 degrees. A right triangle has one 90-degree angle. An obtuse triangle has one angle that is greater than 90 degrees.

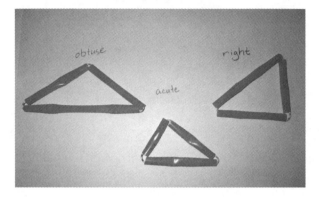

Step 7 (optional): Use a protractor to measure the angles of each different type of triangle. The three interior angles will add up to 180 degrees for any triangle.

The Math Behind It

Any three-sided closed shape is called a triangle. Triangles are classified by their sides and angles. The easiest one to understand is the equilateral triangle; with three equal sides, the angles are forced to be equal. An isosceles triangle has two equal sides and two equal angles. Scalene triangles have three unequal sides and three unequal angles.

All three angles are less than 90 degrees in an acute triangle. Obtuse triangles have one angle that is greater than 90 degrees. Right triangles have one angle that is equal to 90 degrees and can be either scalene or isosceles. The three interior angles of a triangle, no matter which kind of triangle, always add up to 180 degrees.

Triangles are an incredibly important shape in our world. Rafter trusses, cell phone towers, and ladders are all examples of useful triangles. Look around you for even more triangles.

Math for the Ages

Triangles are taught at a very young age, so this is a great early activity. Safety scissors will cut straws, so this could be done even with preschoolers. Elementary students will better remember the types of triangles by building them rather than just seeing them. The option of measuring the angles with a protractor is a great way to reinforce the 180-degree rule. Math is often a strictly paper-and-pencil subject, but this activity gets students involved.

Right triangles are at the heart of physics and many engineering branches, like civil and mechanical engineering. High school teachers can use this activity to help teach sine, cosine, and tangent. Even my high school students appreciate the hands-on element of learning.

Thumbs Up

Measure the height of something in the distance by using your thumb and a tape measure.

Geometry Concepts: Isosceles right triangles and similar triangles

From the Junk Drawer:

☐ Your thumb   ☐ Friend
☐ Tape measure

Step 1: Find a tall, distant object to measure and have a friend stand next to it. Extend your arm, make a fist, and point your thumb straight up. Look at the distant object, aligning the bottom of your fist to its base. Move forward or backward until the top of your thumb lines up with the top of the tall object.

Step 2: Rotate your fist sideways, making sure you keep the bottom of your fist on the object's base (but perpendicular to it). Have your friend start walking away from the object in the same direction your thumb is pointing. Yell at him or her to stop when just lined up with the end of your thumb. Meet your friend where he or she is standing and measure the distance from your friend to the base of the tall object. That distance is the same as the height of the tall object.

The Math Behind It

The tall object's height and the distance your friend traveled are the same because you created an isosceles right triangle. It is a right triangle because your thumb was perpendicular to itself in Steps 1 and 2. It is an isosceles triangle because your thumb is the same length in both directions. The triangle created by rotating your thumb in Steps 1 and 2 is the same triangle at a smaller proportion (called a similar triangle) to the triangle created by the tall object and your friend.

Math for the Ages

This lab is suitable for all ages. A tall building, flagpole, utility pole, or light pole on a sports field all work well for a school lab, and you can probably find someone at the school who knows the actual height of the object. Another option is to try one or two of the other indirect methods shown in this book and compare values.

Trig Function Coffee Filter

Use a coffee filter to verify the basic trigonometry functions.

Geometry Concepts: Sine, cosine, and tangent

From the Junk Drawer:

☐ Coffee filter (or cheap paper plates or round paper)

☐ Marker

☐ Ruler

☐ Calculator

Step 1: Fold a coffee filter in half. Make sure the edges line up perfectly. Crease the edge with a thumbnail. Fold the coffee filter again to make a quarter, then crease the edge.

Step 2: Unfold the coffee filter. Mark the center with an *O* for origin. Mark a dot where the fold touches the top outer edge of the coffee filter and label it *A*. Put a dot where the crease touches the right outer edge of the coffee filter and label it *B*.

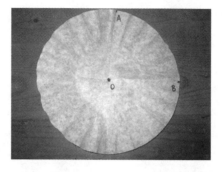

Step 3: Fold the *A* down until it just touches the *O* at the center. Make sure the fold is parallel to the equator (the horizontal crease in the center of the coffee filter). Crease this new fold with your thumbnail.

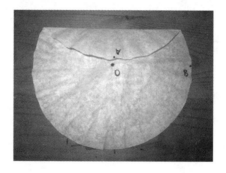

Step 4: Unfold the coffee filter again. Label the point where the fold-line you just made touches the edge of the coffee filter with the letter *C*, as shown.

Step 5: Draw a line connecting *O* to *C* using a ruler and a marker. Draw a second line to connect *O* to *B* in the same manner. To make a right triangle, draw a perpendicular line down from *C* to the line *OB* as shown. Draw a small rectangle in the right-angle corner you just drew to show that it is a 90-degree angle. We know that angle *COB* is a 30-degree angle because of trigonometry, but we are going to verify that.

Label the opposite, adjacent, and hypotenuse sides of the triangle. The opposite side is called that because it is opposite the 30-degree angle. The adjacent side is called that because it is adjacent (next) to the 30-degree angle. The hypotenuse is the longest side of the triangle.

Now you can verify that the sine of any angle (θ), of a right triangle, is equal to the length of the opposite side (*a*) divided by the length of the hypotenuse (*c*): $\sin \theta = a \div c$. Measure the hypotenuse and opposite sides. Make sure your calculator is set for degrees, then put the lengths into the calculator and you will see that the sine of 30 degrees is 0.5. The cosine of any angle (of a right triangle) is equal to the length of the adjacent side (*b*) divided by the length of the hypotenuse: $\cos \theta = b \div c$. Using a calculator, you will see the cosine of 30 degrees is equal to 0.866. Measure both the adjacent side and the hypotenuse and verify the cosine calculation.

You can also try the tangent of 30 degrees, which is equal to the opposite side divided by the adjacent side.

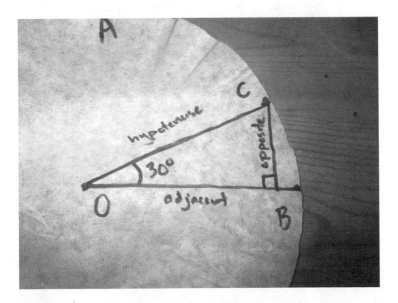

Step 6: You can also create a 60-degree angle using the other side of the coffee filter. Fold the left half until the left edge reaches point O. Make sure the fold is parallel to the vertical fold down the center that you made in Step 1.

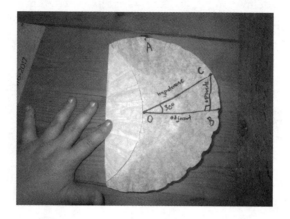

Step 7: Unfold the coffee filter. Label the top point E where the crease meets the edge of the filter. Mark the point where the equator fold reaches this fold as point F.

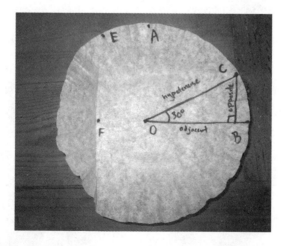

Step 8: Draw a complete right triangle by connecting points O, F, and E. When you label the sides this time, be careful. Hypotenuse is still the longest side. The opposite side is the side opposite the 60-degree angle as shown and the adjacent side is next to the 60-degree angle. Follow the math in Step 5 to verify that the angle is 60 degrees. You can also make

the drawing less busy by abbreviating opposite (opp.), adjacent (adj.), and hypotenuse (hyp.). Eventually, you will probably just use O, A, and H to label the sides.

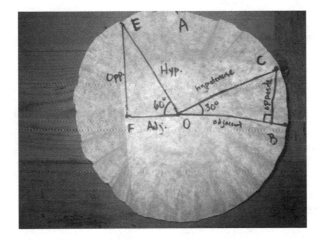

The Math Behind It

The basic trigonometry functions for right triangles are sine, cosine, and tangent, which are just ratios of the sides of the triangle. A helpful way to remember this is SOH-CAH-TOA. The sine (S) of the angle is equal to the opposite (O) side divided by the hypotenuse (H)—SOH. The cosine (C) of the angle (A) is equal to the adjacent side divided by the hypotenuse (H)—CAH. And the tangent (T) of the angle is equal to the opposite side (O) divided by the adjacent (A)—TOA.

By folding the coffee filter down in Step 2, you are ensuring that the opposite side is exactly one-half of the hypotenuse, since you were dividing the vertical radius in half. The radius of a circle will always be the hypotenuse of the triangle. This will work for any size circular object, like your coffee filter or a paper plate. So one-half of the radius (opposite) divided by the entire radius (hypotenuse) is always going to be 0.5. And the sine of 30 degrees is 0.5.

For the second triangle, you are repeating the same fold, but since it is vertical, you ensure the adjacent side of the second triangle is one-half of the radius. And cosine is equal to adjacent divided by the hypotenuse ($C = A \div H$). And the cosine of 60 degrees is equal to 0.5 also.

Sine, cosine, and tangent work for any angles of a right triangle. Right-triangle trigonometry is fundamental to engineering, math, and architecture.

Math for the Ages

Right-triangle trigonometry is usually something encountered in high school, but elementary students could easily do the math in this activity with a little help. Even preschoolers could create the triangles and have fun doing so, but the math might be a little over their heads.

Wheat Cracker Area

Compare area to perimeter with wheat crackers.

Geometry Concepts: Area and perimeter

From the Junk Drawer:

☐ Paper

☐ Tape (optional)

☐ Pencil or marker

☐ 12 square wheat crackers (or square cheese crackers)

Step 1: On a long sheet of paper (or two smaller sheets taped together), draw a vertical and a horizontal arrow perpendicular to each other. Label the vertical arrow L for length and the horizontal arrow W for width.

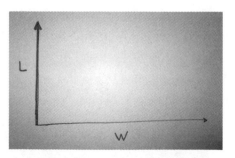

Step 2: Inside your arrows, place a rectangle of wheat crackers with a width of 1 cracker and a length of 12 crackers. The area of the rectangle is 12

crackers. The perimeter is the number of outside edges (those sides that are not touching other crackers). You should have 26 edges.

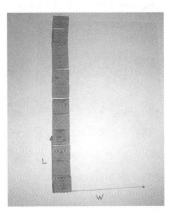

Step 3: Now rearrange your crackers to create a rectangle with a width of 2 crackers and a length of 6 crackers. How many crackers make up the rectangle? How many outside edges are there?

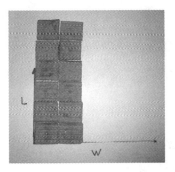

Step 4: Rearrange your crackers to create a rectangle with a width of 3 crackers and a length of 4 crackers. How many crackers make up the rectangle? How many outside edges are there ?

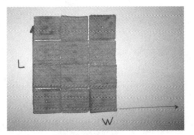

Step 5: Rearrange your crackers again to create a rectangle with a width of 4 crackers and a length of 3 crackers. How many wheat crackers make up the rectangle? How many outside edges are there ?

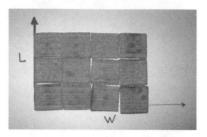

Step 6: Now for the final shape: rearrange your crackers to create a rectangle with a width of 6 crackers and a length of 2 crackers. How many crackers make up the rectangle? How many outside edges are there? (If the activity is done on clean paper, you can safely eat the crackers at the end of the lab.)

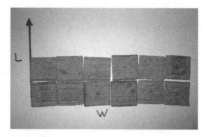

The Math Behind It

Area is almost always measured in square units, like square feet, square yards, square centimeters, and so on. The area of a rectangle is length times width ($A = l \times w$), and in this activity the area was always 12 crackers. Perimeter is the distance along the outside of a shape and is always measured in a linear distance, like feet, yards, centimeters, and so on. The perimeter was measured in edges of the cracker for this lab.

There is a formula for finding the perimeter of a rectangle—see if you can figure out what it is. An easy way to think of the difference between area and perimeter is to look at a fenced-in area. The area is the number of square feet (or yards) inside the fencing. Perimeter is the length of the fence surrounding the area.

Math for the Ages

This activity is suitable for all ages. It is a great way to introduce square units. The crackers give students a tangible square unit to use. Even high school students still struggle with the concept that area is in square units and perimeter is in linear units. This lab will help them internalize the difference. It also makes a great inquiry lab to discover the formula for the perimeter of a rectangle ($2l + 2w$). Perimeter can then be linked to circle circumference if circumference has been covered in previous lessons. You could research real-world situations for which you would want the largest possible perimeter for an area and those for which you would want the smallest possible perimeter for an area.

Diameter of the Sun

Use an index card to find a bright fact on a sunny day.

Geometry Concept: Similar triangles

From the Junk Drawer:

- ☐ Thumbtack or pin
- ☐ 2 index cards
- ☐ Pen or marker
- ☐ Meter stick
- ☐ Friend
- ☐ Scrap paper
- ☐ Calculator

Step 1: Use a thumbtack or pin to poke a small hole in the first index card on a sunny day.

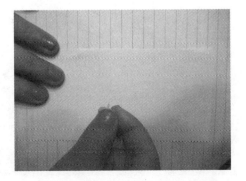

Step 2: With a pen or marker, draw two parallel lines 1 centimeter apart on the other index card. Go outdoors if you aren't already and stand in the sunlight.

Step 3: Hold an index card in each hand so that the cards face one another. Move the card with the pinhole up and down in the sunlight until a small image of the sun (a bright dot) appears in the shadow of the index card in your other hand. Move the index card with the hole until the image of the sun is exactly the same size as the distance between the two lines. This is the most critical measurement and hardest to get, so be patient.

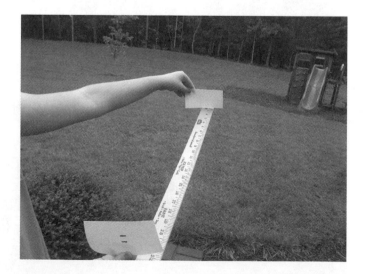

Step 4: Hold the index cards in place while a friend uses a meter stick to measure the distance between the cards in centimeters. Write the distance down on a piece of scrap paper. The triangle formed from the card to the ground is similar to the triangle formed from the sun to the card.

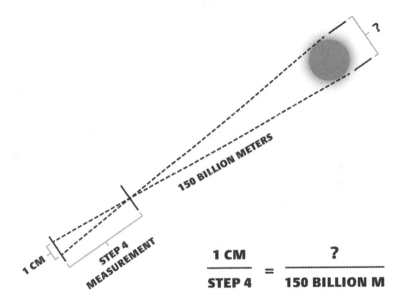

$$\frac{1 \text{ CM}}{\text{STEP 4}} = \frac{?}{150 \text{ BILLION M}}$$

Step 5: Set up the formula as shown. Convert all of the units to meters. To convert centimeters to meters, simply divide by 100. The average distance between the earth and the sun is 149.6 billion meters. Solve the equation for the unknown diameter of the sun. You can leave the billion out when you put it into your calculator—your answer will just be that many billions of meters.

The Math Behind It

Light travels in straight lines. The triangle formed by the sun image on one card and the pinhole on the other card is similar to the triangle formed by the sun and the pinhole. You have two very skinny isosceles triangles known as similar triangles. Similar triangles have equal angles and the ratio of two sides is the same for both triangles. So the ratio of the sun image's diameter to the card distance is equal to the sun's actual diameter to the card-to-sun distance. The unknown sun diameter can be solved for.

Math for the Ages

Remind students to never look at the sun. This activity is suitable for almost any school-age child. Younger children will need more help with the math. Older students may want to use scientific notation for practice. Results within 10 percent of the actual sun's diameter are very good. The diameter of the sun is approximately 1.4 billion meters.

The best thing to do for a classroom is calculate the average of all students' answers. That should make the number closer to the actual diameter and emphasizes the need to repeat an experiment multiple times for accuracy. Students could also repeat the experiment with a variety of image sizes, for example, 1.0, 1.2, 1.4, 1.6 centimeters. Each group would then have multiple measurements with which to calculate.

How Tall Is Your House?

Use your Angle Machine and simple trigonometry to measure your house.

Geometry Concepts: Right triangles and tangent

From the Junk Drawer:

☐ Angle Machine (see page 36)   ☐ Scientific calculator
☐ Tape measure or meter stick

Step 1: Use the Angle Machine you built earlier, or make one now using the instructions on page 36. Go outside and stand far enough from your house (or the object of your choosing) so that you can see both its base and its top. Close one eye and look through the straw of your Angle Machine at the peak of your house. If you live in a flat-roofed building, you could also use a tall tree, flagpole, or light pole. The object you measure needs to have a base you can measure from. For example, a mountain would be impossible to measure using this technique. The angle that the string makes with the protractor is the angle of the house peak above horizontal.

Step 2: Measure the distance from the ground to your eyes with a tape measure or meter stick. In the final step, you will have to add your eye height into your calculation.

Step 3: Measure the distance from your feet to the base of your house.

Step 4: The tangent of an angle is equal to the height of the opposite side (your house's peak) divided by the length of the adjacent side (the distance from where you stood to the base of your house). Your unknown is the house peak height (h). Multiply the tangent of your angle (θ) by the distance from your feet to the base of the house (b): $h = b \times \tan\theta$.

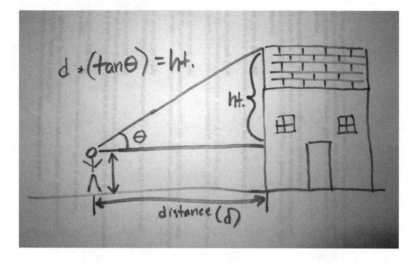

Step 5: The height calculated in Step 4 is the height above the Angle Machine. The last step is to add the height of the Angle Machine (your eye height). Total height = eye height + Step 4 height.

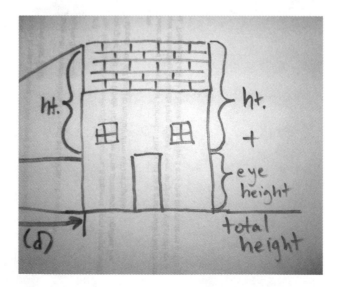

The Math Behind It

The side of your house becomes the opposite side of a right triangle. The distance along the ground from the house to your feet becomes the adjacent side of the right triangle. The trigonometric function tangent is equal to the length of the opposite side divided by the length of the adjacent side. You can solve for the unknown height of the house if you know the angle and the distance along the ground.

One use of this technique is surveying. Surveying is determining the area and location of an object to create a map or scale drawing. Model rocket enthusiasts also use this measurement. The rocketeers sight through the clinometer at the rocket at its highest point. By measuring how far they are from the launch pad, they can solve for the height of the rocket.

Math for the Ages

Right-triangle trigonometry is usually taught in high school, but you can teach it to almost any age with a little help. This lab is a great way to introduce trigonometry and helps you calculate how high your rocket flew.

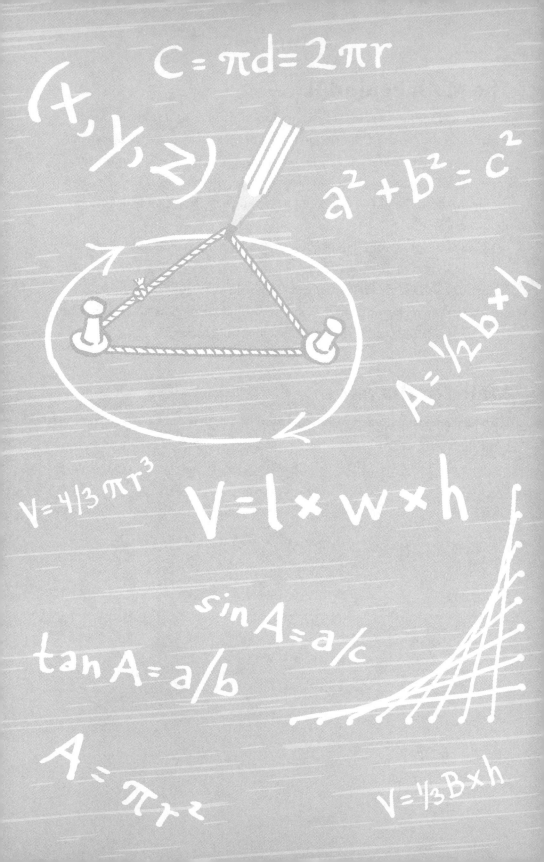

Fun Geometry Activities

M ath needs to be fun. But while math is naturally fun to some people who like the challenge of solving puzzles, others need a little help to make it enjoyable. Winning students over early will help them when they have to learn more boring math concepts. There are parts of every subject that aren't fun to learn, but they have to be learned anyway. Periodically including entertaining activities in your lessons shows young people the joys of math.

Circle Art

Use a compass and pencil to create amazing artwork.

Geometry Concepts: Circles and diameters

From the Junk Drawer:
☐ Compass

☐ Paper or scrap cardboard

☐ Pencil

☐ Ruler

☐ Colored markers, pens, or crayons

Step 1: On the center of a piece of paper or cardboard, draw a circle with a compass and pencil. You can use your Pencil Compass from page 1 or one from a store. Your circle can be almost any size, as long as three circles of the same size will fit across your paper. Cardboard is easier to use for this activity since many compasses have points that work best if stuck into cardboard to anchor the center point.

Step 2: Draw a light line across the diameter of the circle using a ruler. Put the point of the compass at the intersection of the line and the left side of a circle. Draw a second circle that overlaps with the first. Repeat on the right side of the first circle to create a third overlapping circle. After you draw these two circles you can erase the diameter line, or you can leave it if you plan to color the circles.

Step 3: Put the compass point at the new top two intersections shown and draw two more circles (the same size as before) above the three overlapping circles.

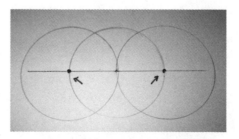

Step 4: Put the compass point at the bottom two intersections shown and draw two more circles (the same size). Once finished, you can color each segment a different color. Have fun and be creative.

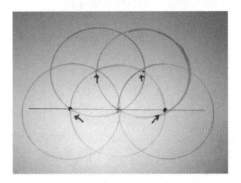

Step 5 (optional): You can extend the pattern by placing the point of the compass at every new intersection created and fill the entire page.

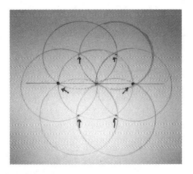

The Math Behind It

The circle is a big part of our everyday life—it's a simple shape that surrounds us. The compass is a very useful tool for drawing circles, and this activity is a fun way to practice using one and to draw a diameter.

Math for the Ages

This activity is appropriate for any age. The youngest set will need help using a compass. This is a great activity even for older kids as brain candy after a really difficult test or lesson. Teaching kids that math can be fun is valuable.

Circle Art 2

Learn the parts of a circle.

Geometry Concepts: Diameters, semicircles, quadrants, arcs, chords, and segments of a circle

From the Junk Drawer:

☐ Compass

☐ Paper

☐ Pencil

☐ Marker

☐ Crayons, markers, or watercolor paints (optional)

Step 1: Draw a large circle in the center of a sheet of paper with a compass and pencil. Draw and label a horizontal diameter across the middle of the circle with a marker and ruler. Label one half of the circle *semicircle*, which is half of a circle.

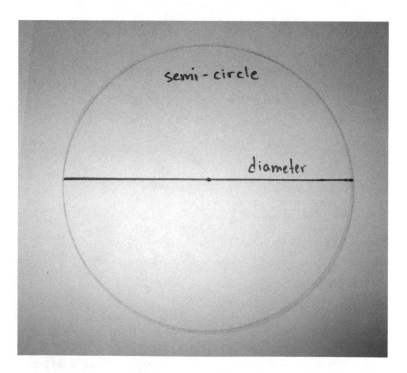

Step 2: Draw another diameter perpendicular to the first. This will separate the circle into four equal parts. Label one of these four parts *quadrant*.

You can also thicken half of one of the diameter lines and label it *radius*. A radius is half of a diameter.

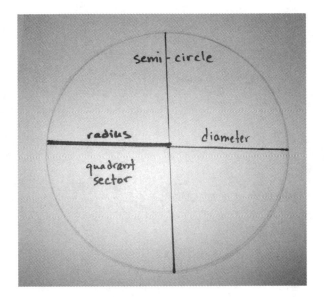

Step 3: Draw a line from one edge of the circle to the other in the unlabeled semicircle. Label this line *chord*. The portion on each side of the circle is called a segment and should be labeled. Finally, thicken part of the edge of the circle. Label this curved part along the edge *arc*.

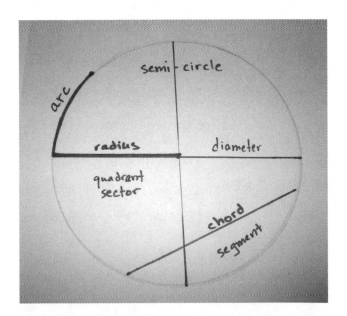

Step 4 (optional): Color each different part with crayons, markers, or watercolor paints. Use light colors so the labels are still visible.

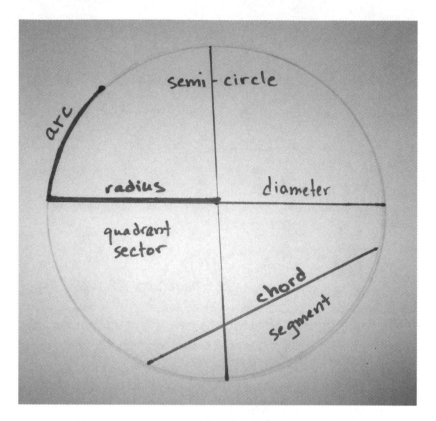

The Math Behind It

Circles are a big part of geometry, and many terms are associated with them. This activity is a great way to internalize terms associated with circles.

Math for the Ages

This activity is perfect for any age. Preschoolers may need help drawing the initial circle with a compass or could trace a round object. In a classroom setting, the leader could do the steps on the board or a projector. Encourage students to draw any arcs, segments, or chords they want. Also remind students to spread all the terms out so their drawings aren't too crowded.

Circles into Squares

Amaze your friends with this fun math trick.

Geometry Concepts: Circles and squares

From the Junk Drawer:

☐ Paper   ☐ Clear tape

☐ Scissors

Step 1: The goal of this activity is to create two strips of paper that are the same size. Fold and crease the edge of one sheet of paper.

Step 2: Cut along the edge that you folded over, as shown.

Step 3: Unfold the strip of paper and cut along the crease. You should have two equal-sized strips of paper.

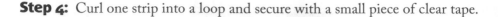

Step 4: Curl one strip into a loop and secure with a small piece of clear tape.

Step 5: Put the other strip through the center of the first loop and secure this second strip into a loop with a small piece of tape.

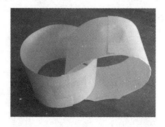

Step 6: Now secure the two loops to each other by reaching inside one and taping it to the other. Flip the loops over and tape the other loop to the first loop. The loops should now be firmly attached to each other.

Step 7: You want to create a slit in the middle of one of the loops. Slightly bend one loop and cut a small slit it. The slit only has to be big enough to insert the point of one of the scissor blades into.

Step 8: Insert one scissor blade into the slit and cut all the way around one loop. Try to keep the scissors in the middle of the loop so you're cutting it evenly in half lengthwise. You should now have three interconnected rings, one fat and two thin.

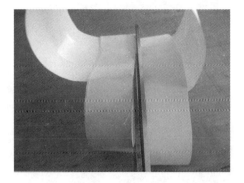

Step 9: Lay your creation down on a flat surface, as shown.

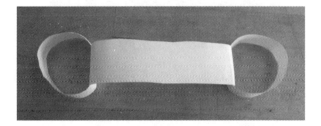

Step 10: Starting at one end of the wide strip, use scissors to completely cut the wide strip. Try to stay in the middle as you cut.

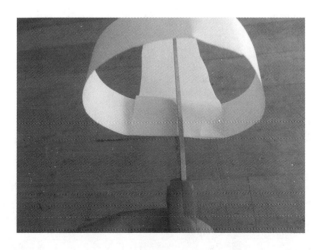

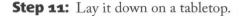

Step 11: Lay it down on a tabletop.

Step 12: Pull the bottom two straight strips out to the sides. Flatten it out. You just turned two circles into a square.

The Math Behind It

This is a fun trick that works because of math. When you cut the first loop, you are creating two circles out of one. These circles are at either end of the other loop. But the other loop has been cut, so it will now lie flat. Splitting the wide strip that remains creates four strips of equal length. When you unroll it, you have a four-sided shape with equal lengths—a square.

Math for the Ages

This activity is safe to do with any children who can use scissors. This is a great way to review circles and squares with younger children. A fun challenge is to have all the students create the two interlocked loops with your help and securely tape them. Then have them figure out how to turn the circles into a square on their own. This makes them think independently and thinking critically is good.

This is a great activity for Friday afternoon when you finish your lesson five minutes early. Most children will love to show off to their parents or friends. Remember: to teach them, you have to reach them. Fun activities like this make some of the more boring activities a little easier to swallow.

Curved Yarn

Use leftover card stock and yarn to create a parabola with only straight lines.

Geometry Concept: Parabolas

From the Junk Drawer:

- ☐ Marker
- ☐ Ruler
- ☐ File folder or empty cereal box
- ☐ Pushpin
- ☐ Paper clip
- ☐ Yarn
- ☐ Scissors
- ☐ Tape

Step 1: Use a marker and ruler to make eight dots that are 1 centimeter apart across an old file folder. This is a perfect use for old file folders, but any type of heavier card stock material would work, like old cereal boxes. On the right side of the file folder, mark eight dots that are 1 centimeter apart going up from the last bottom dot. The two rows of dots should be perpendicular to each other.

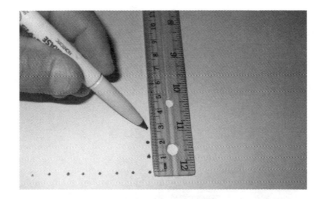

Step 2: Use a pushpin to punch a hole at each dot. Wiggle the pin around to make the hole large enough to get the yarn through.

Step 3: Unfold a paper clip so the metal is straight. If paper clip breaks, that is OK—you only need a straight piece to help thread the yarn through the holes. Take the straight part of the clip and stick it through the holes to make the holes even larger.

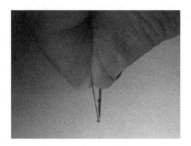

Step 4: Cut at least 3 meters (or 1 yard) of colorful yarn. Tie a very large knot in one end. You might need to tie several knots together to make it larger. You want the knot large enough that it will not pull through the holes you created.

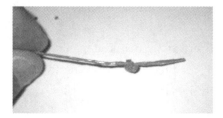

Step 5: Securely tape the unknotted end of the yarn to the straight piece of the paper clip. Push the paper clip end of the yarn through the bottom left hole from the backside of the file folder.

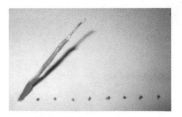

Step 6: Pull the yarn all the way through until the knot stops it. Push the yarn through the first hole up on the right vertical line of holes.

Step 7: Pull the yarn tight.

Step 8: Pull the yarn from the vertical line of holes back to the horizontal line of holes, and thread it from the back of the file folder through to the front of the second hole from the left.

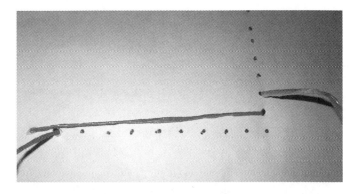

Step 9: Pull it tight. Continue repeating the pattern until you have used all the holes.

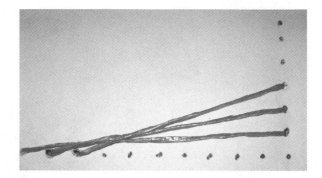

Step 10: The finished Curved Yarn should look like this image. Tie a large knot behind the file folder when you reach the last hole and use scissors to trim off any excess.

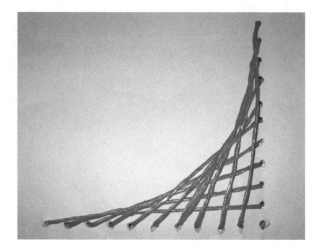

The Math Behind It

Curved Yarn is a project in string art. String art is using straight pieces of string to create curves. The simple curve you created is one half of a parabola. A parabola is a function of y being equal to a value time x squared.

String art became popular in the 1970s but is still fun today and it can help you learn math. It is also a great way to add an art component to math.

Math for the Ages

With pushpins and paper clips, this activity is suitable for elementary age students and up. Students may really enjoy making this string art and can search online for other string-art designs. String art is traditionally done with wooden boards and nails instead of the card stock–and-yarn method outlined here. A great high school–level tie-in is to explain that each straight line of yarn represents a tangent to the curve at that point. This is a great introduction to the concept of a derivative in a calculus course, since the derivative is the slope of a tangent line at that point.

Flip-Book Fun

Create flip-books using geometric shapes.

Geometry Concept: Shapes

From the Junk Drawer:
☐ Pack of small sticky notes   ☐ Marker
☐ Pencil

Step 1: For flip-books, you can use a pack of sticky notes or simply cut and staple small sheets of same-sized paper together. Decide what you want to draw for your flip-book first; a bouncing ball, a square that grows into a rectangle, or a shrinking circle are all easy images to start with, but you can let your creativity run wild. Start by drawing your first picture on the top page.

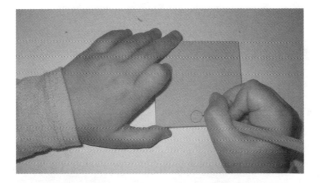

Step 2: Draw your next picture on the second page. It needs to be moved slightly or grow a little depending on what you plan to animate. Hint: if you press hard with your pencil while drawing, it will leave a slight impression on the next sheet that you can use as a reference to start from. Continue to draw your object on each sequential page, making sure to move it slightly on each sticky note.

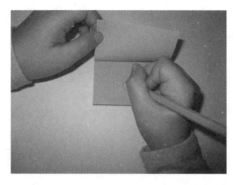

Step 3: Hold the flip-book in one hand and flip through the pages with the other hand. This technique will take some practice to master, but you can do it. When finished, flip the pack of paper over and draw another animation. Don't throw the sticky notes out when you're done drawing; they will still work for notes.

The Math Behind It

Flip-books work because of the way our brains perceive images. When you look at something, an image forms on the retina of our eye and then is processed by the brain. Your brain captures that image and holds on to it for up to one-tenth of a second. This is called persistence of vision, and it is the reason you barely perceive that you've blinked your eyes. In television and in your flip-book, a new image replaces the old image before your brain forgets the old image. You see a seamless transition from one object to the next. Flip-books are a fun way to explore geometric shapes.

Math for the Ages

My daughter started making flip-books before elementary school, so all ages can make these. The topics may need to be geared toward the age of the students. This is a great Fun Math Friday activity. Adding a little fun to math might help students enjoy the subject even more.

Freehand Circles

Draw near-perfect circles every time with nothing but a pencil.

Geometry Concept: Circles

From the Junk Drawer:

☐ Pencil   ☐ Paper

Step 1: The key to doing this is to keep your hand still and spin the paper. Hold a pencil as you normally would in your writing hand. To draw a medium-size circle, place your bent pinky against the paper. Do not press so hard that the paper can't spin.

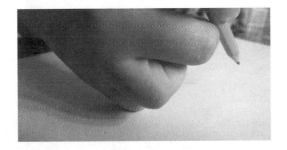

Step 2: Practice spinning the paper around a few times with your nonwriting hand. Now put the pencil lead down along with your pinky finger. Do not move your writing hand at all. Spin the paper around, and you will have a perfect circle. It takes practice to hold the pencil and your writing fingers still. You can do it.

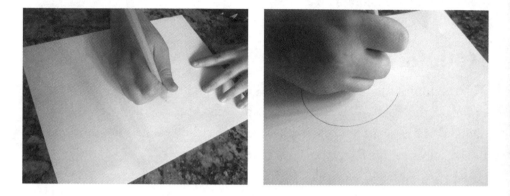

Step 3: For a smaller circle, put your ring (or middle) finger down and spin the paper around that.

The Math Behind It

Every circle has a center. The center of the circle is directly below the part of your hand that touches it. The pencil doesn't move and the paper spins freely about the pivot point. This takes a little practice, but is a fun trick you can use your entire life.

Math for the Ages

This activity is perfect for almost all ages. It just takes practice. The youngest set may struggle to hold the pencil still; crayons may be a good choice for them.

Magnet Shapes

Use magnets to learn shapes.

Math Concepts: Equal-sided shapes

From the Junk Drawer:

☐ 6 small, round, strong magnets   ☐ Glue

☐ White correction fluid (optional)   ☐ Bowl of water

☐ 6 plastic bottle caps   ☐ Pencil

Step 1: First test the magnets you've selected to find which sides of the magnets repel each other. Lay one magnet down and place another magnet next to it. Push one magnet toward the other. If it attracts the other magnet, turn it over. Repeat for all six magnets until they each repel the rest. You can mark them with white correction fluid if you choose, but make sure not to turn any over.

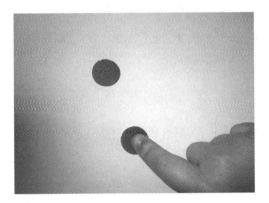

Step 2: Place each magnet in the open side of a plastic bottle cap. Be careful to keep them all turned the same way they were in Step 1. Glue the magnets in the caps if you want extra stability.

Step 3: Fill a bowl with water. Float three bottle caps on the water—they should repel each other. You may need to push one with a pencil if it sticks to the side, but this is rare. The three caps will form the vertices of an equilateral triangle.

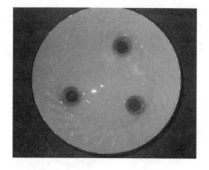

Step 4: Add a fourth bottle cap to the water and use the pencil to push the cap to one side of the bowl. The other caps will move until the caps form the vertices of a square.

Step 5: Add a fifth cap and push it toward one side of the bowl to form a regular **pentagon**.

Step 6: For a fun challenge, try putting the sixth cap in the center of the pentagon. This is difficult and sometimes takes many tries. Experiment and try to create other shapes and challenges.

The Math Behind It

Magnets have north and south poles. Like-poles repel. Two north poles will repel each other, and two south poles will too. Since all the caps will repel each other, they create the corners (vertices) of equal-sided shapes. Equilateral triangles, squares, and regular pentagons all have equal-length sides.

I started using this as an activity to introduce magnet repulsion when I first noticed the shapes. Even high school students enjoy this activity.

Math for the Ages

This activity is perfect for all ages. Small magnets can be salvaged from broken refrigerator magnets or bought in the craft aisles of dollar stores or big-box stores. For a classroom setting, keeping a set of bottle-cap magnets is a great idea. One side of my filing cabinet is filled with these, and students have fun creating art or spelling words.

Math Triangles

Have fun by solving this challenging little puzzle.

Geometry Concepts: Triangles, critical thinking

From the Junk Drawer:

☐ Pencil

☐ Paper

☐ 6 poker chips, bottle caps, or paper

circles

☐ Scissors

☐ Marker

Step 1: Use a pencil to draw a large triangle on a sheet of paper. Draw a circle at each **vertex** of the triangle. You can trace around a bottle cap or a poker chip if that is what you are using for playing pieces, or you can simply draw the circles freehand. If you aren't using bottle caps or poker chips, cut six circles out of paper that are the same size as the circles you've drawn.

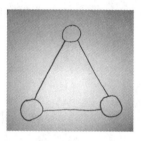

Step 2: Draw three more circles that are the same size as your playing chips in the middle of each side of the triangle. Now write the numbers 1, 2, 3, 4, 5, and 6 on the playing circles (or bottle caps, or poker chips). Only one number on each, and don't repeat numbers.

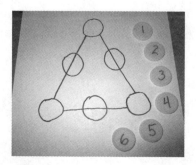

Step 3: To complete the magic triangle, place the pieces on the drawn circles until the sum of the numbers on each side are equal to the same value. One correct solution is shown, but there is more than one number combination that will work.

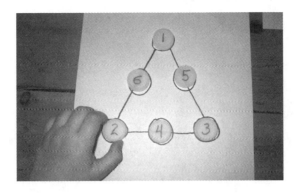

Step 4: For fun, and a bigger challenge, you can create triangles with any number of circles on each side, as long as you have the same number of circles on each side. You also need to have consecutive numbers up to the total number of circles drawn on your playing pieces. Be warned, as the triangles get bigger, the solutions become much more difficult.

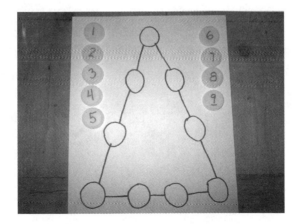

The Math Behind It

Puzzles are a great way to teach critical thinking. The geometry in this activity is light, but the activity is still loads of fun.

Math for the Ages

This is a fun activity for younger children, and older children will love the challenge of solving larger triangles. All of the triangles also have multiple solutions, so keep searching for more answers. If you use old poker chips or bottle caps, you can store those in a plastic bag for future fun. The sheets can also be stored for future attempts too.

Mobius Index Card

Create a crazy shape to fool your friends.

Geometry Concept: Critical thinking

From the Junk Drawer:

- ☐ Blank index card (no lines on either side)
- ☐ Scissors
- ☐ Ruler
- ☐ Pencil

Step 1: Start with a blank index card. Use scissors to cut from one long edge directly into the middle point of the card. Be careful to stop precisely at the middle point. A helpful hint: lay a ruler down the center of the card and make a light mark with a pencil that you can erase after making the cut.

Step 2: On the other side of the card, cut two slits, each one-third of the distance from the end of the card. Be careful to only cut to the exact middle of the card each time. All three cuts should stop directly in the center.

Step 3: Grab the card with your fingers as shown. You are going to twist one-half of the card in the next step, and it takes some practice to get your hands right.

Step 4: Grab one end as shown and gently twist it 180 degrees.

Step 5: Place the card on a table as shown and make the folds sharp. It usually takes a few tries to really get good at it. These make great name cards for teachers to have students use the first few weeks of school as you learn all of the students' names. Pictured are a top view and a side view of the finished Mobius Card.

Now ask a friend who has not watched you create the card, "Which side is the top surface and which is the bottom?" Look at the part standing straight up. "Are both sides the top? How can that be?"

The Math Behind It

Our brains think very logically. Seeing the card cut and twisted in that way fools us into thinking it is impossible to make. A card with lines on one side would clearly show the secret. Share this with your parents, teachers, and friends.

Math for the Ages

This activity is perfect for almost any age, provided the students can cut straight. This is a great classroom, Sunday school, or after-school activity. My students do this day one and write their name on the stand-up part of the Mobius Index Card. They put these cards on their desks for the first few days, which helps me learn their names much faster. This activity also works well with paper, but you may want to cut full sheets into four parts to save trees.

Mobius Strip

Create a crazy shape with only one side.

Geometry Concept: Unique geometry trick

From the Junk Drawer:

☐ Scissors   ☐ Cellophane tape
☐ Paper   ☐ Pencil or pen

Step 1: Cut a long, thin strip of paper. Bring the two short ends of the strip together, gently twisting one end a half turn without creasing the paper.

Step 2: Tape the ends together using cellophane tape as shown to create a crazy shape that only has one side and one edge.

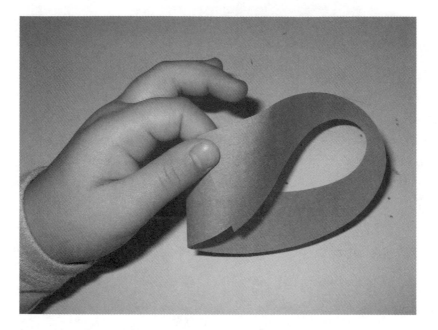

Step 3: Use a pencil or pen to draw a line in the middle of the strip. Keep the pencil in the same place and slowly move the strip around.

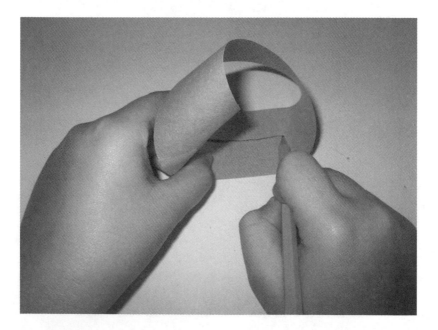

Step 4: Use the point of a pair of scissors to make a small cut on the line in the middle of the strip. Continue cutting all the way along the line. Did you expect what you were left with? It surprises everyone the first time they do it.

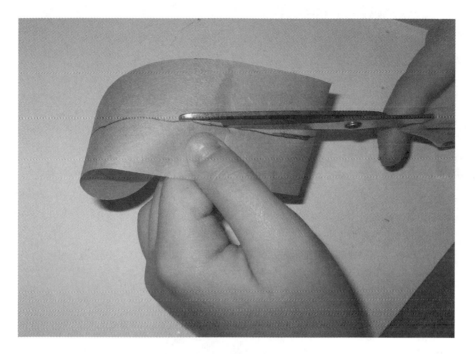

The Math Behind It

The Mobius strip was discovered by August Möbius, a German mathematician in the 1800s. The strange strip only has one side and one edge. Some math-heads refer to this shape as a twisted **cylinder**, but by any name, the strip is just cool. And it is useful. Some conveyor belts are designed as Mobius strips because the belt wears evenly and lasts longer. Old typewriter ribbons and recording tape often used the same shape.

Math for the Ages

This fun activity is perfect for all ages. Young children may need help with the scissors.

Paper Cones, Toilet Paper Tubes, and Flashlight Cones

Use paper cups to learn about sections.

Geometry Concepts: **Conic** sections, cylinder sections, and planes

From the Junk Drawer:

☐ Paper cone cups (or paper to make them)

☐ Tape

☐ Scissors

☐ Toilet paper tubes

☐ Flashlight

Step 1: The first few steps can be done with a paper cone cup, which are commonly used for water coolers. If you don't have paper cone cups, make your own cone by rolling a piece of paper up and adding tape to hold it in place.

Step 2: Use scissors to cut directly across the nose of the paper cone. The end of the cut cone creates what is called a conic section.

Step 3: The section created by this perpendicular cut is a circle. Because the scissors have to pinch the paper to cut it, you are left with an uneven *V* shape where the scissors cut. A true conic section is created with a large flat plane intersecting a cone. When this happens, you don't actually get a *V* in the shape.

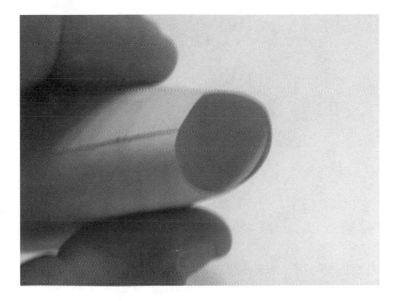

Step 4: Now cut the cone at some angle making sure you cut all the way across the cone.

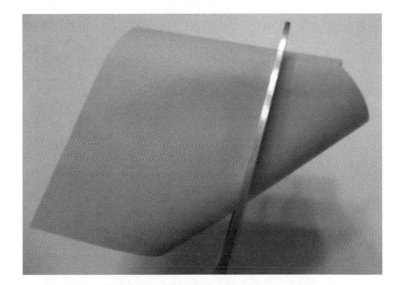

Step 5: The shape of this section is an **ellipse**. Again, because of the scissors, it will still have a small *V* on one side. A perfect ellipse would not have the *V*, but yours is very close.

Step 6: Now create the same shapes with a toilet paper tube. The tube represents a cylinder. The end of the cylinder is already a circle and would represent a plane intersecting the cylinder. Cut across the cylinder at an angle with the scissors.

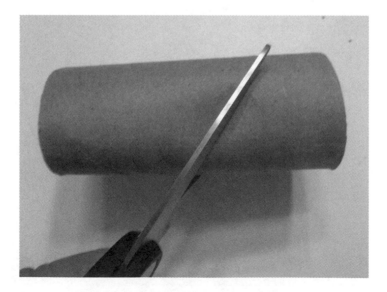

Step 7: The section that you are left with is an ellipse again. As with the cone, the small *V* created by the scissors would not be there in a true section.

Step 8: Another way to see these shapes is to use a flashlight in a dark room. The flashlight will create a cone. Shine it directly at a wall while keeping the flashlight perpendicular to the wall. The section created is a circle. The wall represents a plane and the flashlight creates the cone. Angle the flashlight and you will see an ellipse. Turn it completely parallel to the wall and you can create a parabola. Try this in a dark room—it works!

The Math Behind It

A section is the shape created when a plane intersects a three-dimensional shape, like a cone or cylinder. A plane, in geometry, is a completely flat surface that goes on forever. By varying that angle and the intersection points, you can create circles and ellipses. Two other sections created are parabolas and **hyperbolas**, but the *V* created by the scissors is more pronounced.

Math for the Ages

Sections are taught in high school geometry and above, but it is a very easy concept to understand. This activity is a great way to talk about cones, cylinders, and planes.

Paper Folding 101

Learn facts about lines from folded paper.

Geometry Concepts: **Intersecting lines, vertical angle theorem, congruent**

From the Junk Drawer:

☐ Scrap paper   ☐ Protractor
☐ Pencil

Step 1: Fold a piece of scrap paper as shown and crease the fold with your thumbnail.

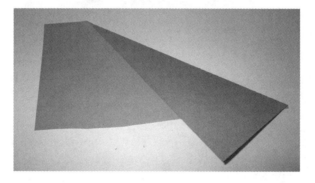

Step 2: Unfold the paper. Then create a second fold, this time folding upward from the bottom of the paper. Crease the second fold with your thumbnail. Unfold the paper and you have created two intersecting lines (that is, two nonparallel lines that can intersect at only one point). You can label the point where the lines intersect with a *P* using a pencil. You can also darken the creases with a pencil.

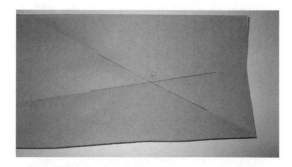

Step 3: Vertical angles are angles created by intersecting lines and are not adjacent to each other, as shown. The vertical angles are equal to each other. Measure them with your protractor to verify that the vertical angles are equal.

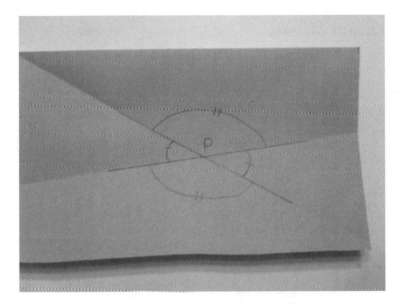

The Math Behind It

Any two lines will only intersect at one point, unless they are parallel. Parallel lines never intersect. The intersecting lines create two sets of vertical angles. Vertical angles are opposite of each other and not touching. The **vertical angle theorem** states that two vertical angles are congruent, or equal.

Math for the Ages

This lab is perfect for all ages and a great way to introduce the term *congruent*. It is also a great way to practice measuring angles with a protractor. You can even still use the paper to work on later, just write across the lines or erase them entirely. In a classroom, you can trade papers with other students to verify their measurements. Although the angles will be different, the vertical angles will be the same.

Recycled Lines of Symmetry

Empty your recycling bin to learn symmetry.

Geometry Concept: **Lines of symmetry**

From the Junk Drawer:

☐ Recycled paper (or other items)
☐ Scissors
☐ Marker

☐ Ruler
☐ Coffee filter (or circle of recycled paper)

Step 1: Cut various angled shapes (such as triangles, squares, rectangles, parallelograms, etc.) using paper from the recycling bin. Magazines are a fun and colorful choice. Another option is to use card stock, construction paper, or old cereal boxes, but they are harder to fold.

Step 2: Start with the square. Fold it to find lines of symmetry. A **line of symmetry** is a fold in which you have exactly the same size and shape on each side of the fold and the edges perfectly match when folded. A square will have multiple lines of symmetry, as do many shapes. How many can you find on a square? Darken the folds with a marker to show the different

lines of symmetry. A square has a few lines of symmetry that are not pictured—did you find them?

Step 3: Try to find lines of symmetry for all of the shapes you cut and darken the fold lines for each shape. Some shapes will have no lines of symmetry. Triangles can have multiple lines of symmetry, depending on the type of triangle you cut.

Step 4: Now test a circle for its unique properties of symmetry. You can use a flattened, round coffee filter or cut a circle from recycled paper. Fold your circle to find the lines of symmetry. How many did you find?

The Math Behind It

A line of symmetry is sometimes called a mirror line, because both sides mirror each other. All symmetry lines have to run through the middle of the shape. A square has four lines of symmetry. Did you find them all? A rectangle only has two lines of symmetry. Triangles can have three, one, or zero lines of symmetry, depending upon the type of triangle. A circle is a fun shape because it has an infinite number of lines of symmetry.

Math for the Ages

This activity is perfect for all ages, as long as the children are old enough to use scissors.

String Ellipses

Create a perfect ellipse using only string, pushpins, scrap cardboard, and a pencil.

Geometry Concepts: **Major** and **minor axis** of an ellipse, **foci**

From the Junk Drawer:

- ☐ Paper
- ☐ Scrap corrugated cardboard
- ☐ 2 pushpins
- ☐ 6-inch piece of string
- ☐ Pencil
- ☐ Ruler

Step 1: Place a piece of paper on a scrap of cardboard. Push two pushpins through the paper into the cardboard about 2 inches apart. Take a 6-inch piece of string and tie it into a loop. Place the circle of string around the two pushpins.

Step 2: Hook the pencil inside the loop of string. Use the pencil to draw along the loop of string. Keep the pencil tight to the loop of string. The knot may cause a small "hiccup" in your ellipse. Repeat the ellipse several times to create a good-looking version.

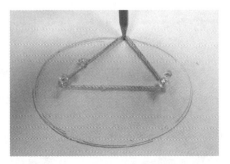

Step 3: Move one of the pins closer and repeat the ellipse drawing. This will create an ellipse with a slightly different shape.

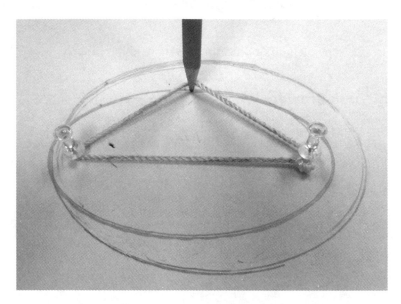

Step 4: Remove the loop of string and the pushpins. With a ruler, draw a straight line connecting both pushpin holes and the end of the long side of the ellipse (for only one of the ellipses). Use a ruler to draw across the shortest part of the middle of the ellipse. Label the long horizontal line *major axis* and the short vertical line *minor axis*.

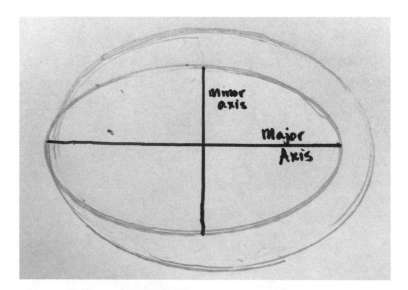

The Math Behind It

An ellipse is a stretched-out circle. A circle has a diameter that is the same anywhere, and a circle has only one center. An ellipse has two foci. The foci are the points where you placed the pushpins. An ellipse has a major and minor axis. The major axis is the longest line you drew across the ellipse. The minor axis is the shortest line.

One practical use of ellipses is to understand the movement of our solar system. The planets actually move in elliptical orbits. The sun is located at one of the foci of the ellipse. The earth is sometimes closer to the sun than at other times, and the crazy thing is, we in the northern hemisphere are closer in the winter. But since the northern hemisphere is tilted away from the sun during the winter, we have colder days.

Math for the Ages

This activity is suitable for all ages. Older students may be led into a greater study of the equations that created the ellipse.

T Puzzle

Create a fun puzzle from geometric shapes.

Geometry Concepts: Shapes and critical thinking

From the Junk Drawer:

☐ Paper   ☐ Pencil or pen

☐ Ruler   ☐ Scissors

Step 1: Draw a 6-inch square on a piece of paper. If you use the corner of the paper, you already have two straight sides from the paper's edges. Once your square is drawn, measure 2 inches down from the top of the paper on both sides and mark with your pencil. Measure 2 inches from each side of the bottom and mark.

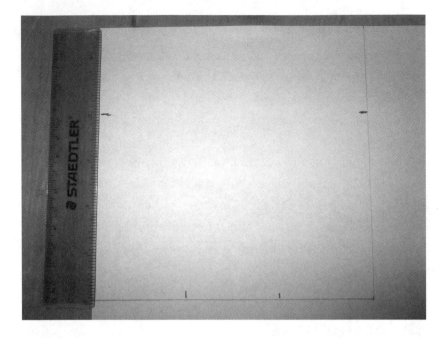

Step 2: Use a pencil or pen to create a *T* using the marks you created. You might want to erase the lines from your original square that don't make up part of the *T*. You don't have to, since you will be cutting that off in the next step anyway.

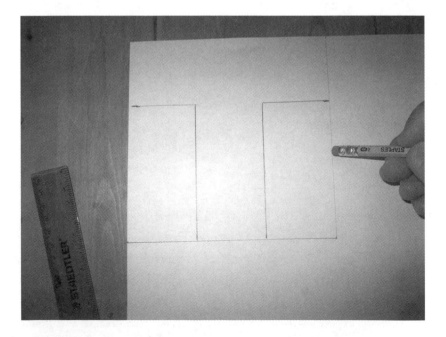

Step 3: Use scissors to cut out the *T*.

Step 4: Connect the top right corner and the right corner of the bottom of the *T* as shown. Use a ruler to darken this line in. The angle of the ruler will be 45 degrees.

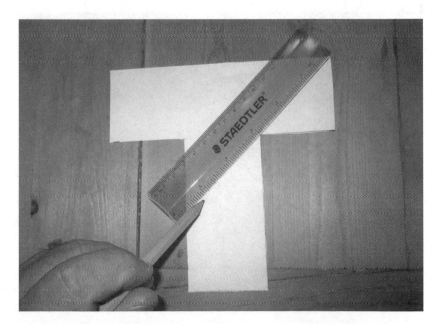

Step 5: Use the ruler to locate the center of the top of the *T*. Make a light mark to indicate the center point.

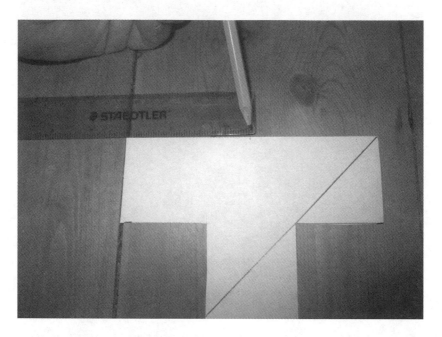

Step 6: Place the ruler at this midpoint of the top and make the ruler parallel with the line you drew in Step 4.

Step 7: Darken the line.

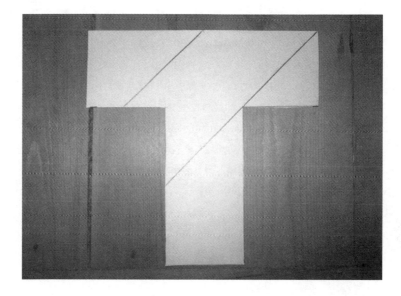

Step 8: Cut along the two darkened lines inside the *T*. You are left with a triangle, an irregular pentagon (five-sided shape), and two right trapezoids. Now the fun starts. Try to make them into shapes without overlapping any paper. Just a few of the shapes you can make are an arrow, a fat *T*, and a pyramid. Solutions are shown on page 175. Experiment and try to make other shapes.

The Math Behind It

Puzzles are a great way to encourage critical thinking. The shapes in the T might be new to you. The biggest shape is an irregular pentagon. All five-sided shapes are called pentagons and this one is irregular because all five sides are different lengths. The most common pentagon is the regular pentagon. Right trapezoids are four-sided figures with two parallel sides and two right angles. And of course, the last piece is a common right triangle.

T Puzzles were actually an advertising gimmick from the early 1900s. The shapes would be printed on the label of a product and people would be asked to cut the pieces out and form a T. Forming the skinny T is easy after you have cut it out but not so easy if you didn't. Our brains struggle to place the irregular pentagon at an angle. Seeing things from different angles is a great way to learn and stretch your brain.

Math for the Ages

This activity is perfect for all ages that can safely use scissors. Teachers or homeschool parents could draw the T for students and just have them cut the shapes out. It is a great activity for encouraging kids to follow directions. If you cut all of the measurements in half to make a 3-inch square, you could fit six T Puzzles on a single piece of printer paper to make copies for a larger group. Another option is to cut the Ts out of old file folders or cereal boxes and store them for future years. This activity could also be done with scrap paper from the recycling bin.

Tangrams

Turn an old cereal box into this ancient Chinese puzzle made from five triangles, a square, and a parallelogram.

Geometry Concepts: Various shapes, **tangrams**, problem-solving

From the Junk Drawer:

☐ Sheet of paper   ☐ Scissors

Step 1: You need a square sheet of paper to start. The entire project can be done with a small, square sticky note for older children. Fold the top right corner of the paper toward the lower left side until the paper forms a right-angle triangle. The top edge of the paper should be flush with the left edge of the paper. Cut off the rectangle that remains beneath the folded triangle and you will have a perfect square.

Step 2: Crease the fold with your thumbnail, then open the paper and cut along the crease. You should now have two triangles.

Step 3: Fold one of the triangles in half and crease the fold with your thumbnail. Unfold the triangle and cut along the fold.

Step 4: The remaining large triangle is going to be cut into five separate shapes. Start by folding the point of the triangle over until it reaches the center of the longest side. Fold, unfold, and then cut along the fold.

Step 5: Fold the long trapezoid directly in the middle and crease the fold. Fold one end triangle over to the center and crease the fold. (Dark lines were added to the photo to show you where the creases are.) Unfold the paper, then cut along the creases to create a square and a small triangle.

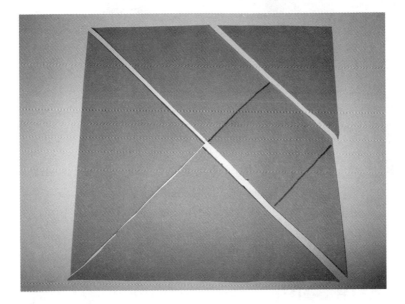

Step 6: Fold the corner of the last piece over until it touches the edge, as shown. Unfold and cut along the fold.

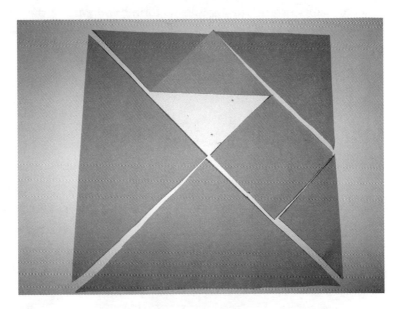

Step 7: The final seven shapes should look like this. Scramble the shapes and try to reassemble the square.

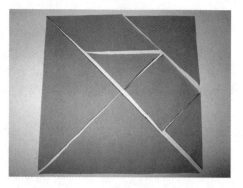

Step 8: There are many figures that can be made from these seven basic shapes. You can see a few solutions on page 176, but you can search online for tangram shapes to find even more. Have fun and be creative. You might be able to make new shapes.

The Math Behind It

Tangrams are a Chinese puzzle that has been popular for hundreds (and possibly thousands) of years. The name in Chinese literally means "seven boards of skill." The seven shapes can be put together to form hundreds of other shapes.

This type of puzzle is called a dissection puzzle or transformational puzzle. These are puzzles of geometric shapes that can transform into new shapes. The puzzles are a fun geometry tool that can help teach basic shapes to students.

Math for the Ages

This activity is suitable for all ages. This is perfect in a classroom setting because the teacher can walk all the students through creating the shapes. The students could write the name of each shape on each piece. Older students could even measure the angle of each vertex and write that on each vertex to review rules on triangles, squares, and parallelograms. Then put an outline of a shape up on the screen and let the students try to make the shape using their tangrams. This is a great puzzle to teach critical thinking skills.

Tessellations Are Fun

Create your own **tessellations** with scrap card stock, scissors, and tape.

Geometry Concepts: Repeating shape patterns

From the Junk Drawer:

☐ Scissors

☐ Card stock, file folder, old cereal
   box, or construction paper

☐ Tape

☐ Ruler

☐ Marker

Step 1: Cut your cardboard into nine rectangles, or more if desired. Into each
rectangle, cut a small triangle.

Step 2: Tape the small triangle to the other side of the rectangle. Repeat for
all of your rectangles, keeping each triangle the same size.

Step 3: Lay the nine shapes out on a table in three rows of three to create a really neat pattern called a tessellation. Experiment with other shapes that tessellate.

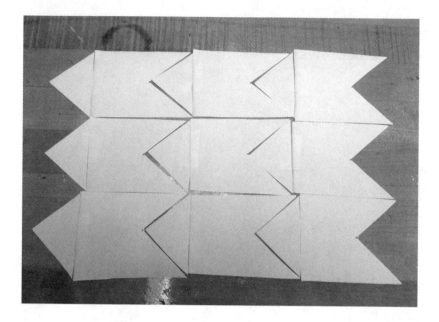

Step 4: Here is another way to create a tessellation. Fold a new piece of paper in half the long way, like a hot dog bun. Then fold it in half the long way again.

Step 5: Unfold the paper and fold it twice horizontally. Your paper should now have 16 squares.

Step 6: Use a ruler and a marker to darken all of the crease lines.

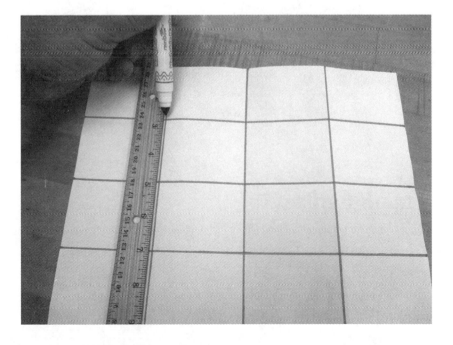

Step 7: Cut the paper into four equal strips. Keep all of the strips lined up.

Step 8: Slide the first and the third strip one half square to the right. This is commonly called a subway tile, because it is a common way to install bricks in a subway. But this subway tiling is also a tessellation. Experiment with other shapes that tessellate.

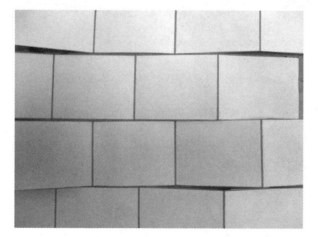

The Math Behind It

Tessellations cover a flat surface with repeating patterns with no overlap. This process is also called tiling, like tile on a bathroom floor. The patterns can be geometric like rectangular subway tiles, but you can also combine two or more different shapes to create tessellations. Squares and triangles make a great combination.

Some artists use tessellations in their artwork. M. C. Escher is probably the best-known tessellation artist, and he would make a great research project for students. Many artists use animals and oddball shapes to tessellate, such as fish. Tessellations also occur in nature—just think about the wax cells in a honeycomb. Tessellations are also behind the concept of quilting to make decorative hangings and bedspreads.

Math for the Ages

This activity is suitable for all ages and is a great way to add an art component to a math class.

Triangular Circle

Turn any circle into a triangle.

Geometry Concepts: Circles and triangles

From the Junk Drawer:

□ Paper plate or coffee filter   □ Pencil or marker
□ Compass (optional)   □ Protractor (optional)

Step 1: The first step requires finding the center of the circle. Paper plates or coffee filters are perfect (and cheap) for this activity, but using a compass and cutting a circle is also good. Fold the circle directly in half, making sure the sides directly match. Fold the half circle over so you are left with a quarter circle. Press hard in the center of the quarter circle.

Step 2: Unfold the circle. Use the pencil or marker to mark the center point. A possible option is to label the fold lines as diameters. Another possible option is to darken half of a diameter and label it as the radius.

Step 3: Fold one segment of the circle over until the edge just reaches the center of the circle. Use a thumbnail to crease the fold. You could open the segment and label the fold line as a chord if you chose.

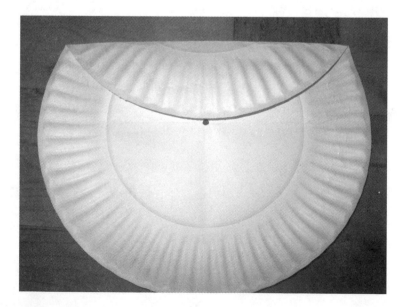

Step 4: Fold the next segment over until the edge just reaches the center. Make sure the end of this second segment perfectly matches up with end of your first segment in a point. Use your thumbnail to crease the fold.

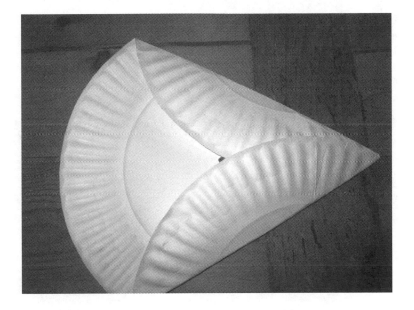

Step 5: Fold the final segment over until the edge just reaches the center to complete your triangle. Use your thumbnail to crease the fold. You now have a perfect equilateral triangle.

Step 6: Open the folds back up into a circle. Darken the fold lines, and label all the interior angles with 60 degrees. All of the side lengths will also be the same length.

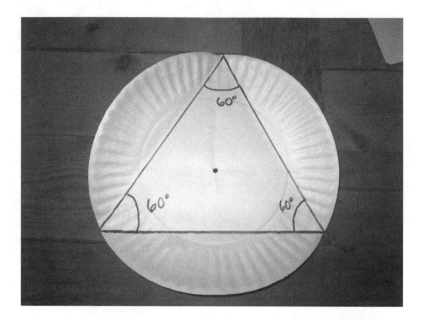

Step 7 (optional): You could fold your equilateral triangle in half. You are left with two 30-60-90 triangles, which you can label as shown.

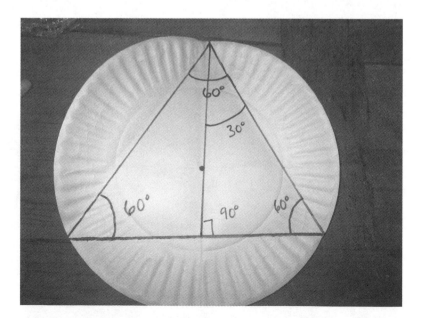

The Math Behind It

Any two diameters will cross at the center of a circle. Folding the edges into the center creates three equal-length chords. The chords are actually the sides of your equilateral triangle. Three equal-length sides inside a circle will always create a perfect equilateral triangle.

Math for the Ages

With the youngest set, just creating the triangle is probably enough, and they may need some adult help. You get to emphasize two shapes: the circle and the triangle. This activity is also a great way to introduce diameter and possibly radius to young kids.

Elementary students should be able to do the folding themselves. They might want to label diameters, center, and at least one radius.

Older elementary students should be introduced to the concept of an equilateral triangle, chords, and segments. They could also use a protractor to measure the interior angles of the triangle and verify that they are all 60 degrees.

Middle and high school students will enjoy this as a Fun Math Friday activity. They should be able to label all the parts. Upper-level students could be asked to determine the length of a chord and the area of the triangle, if you give them only the diameter of the circle.

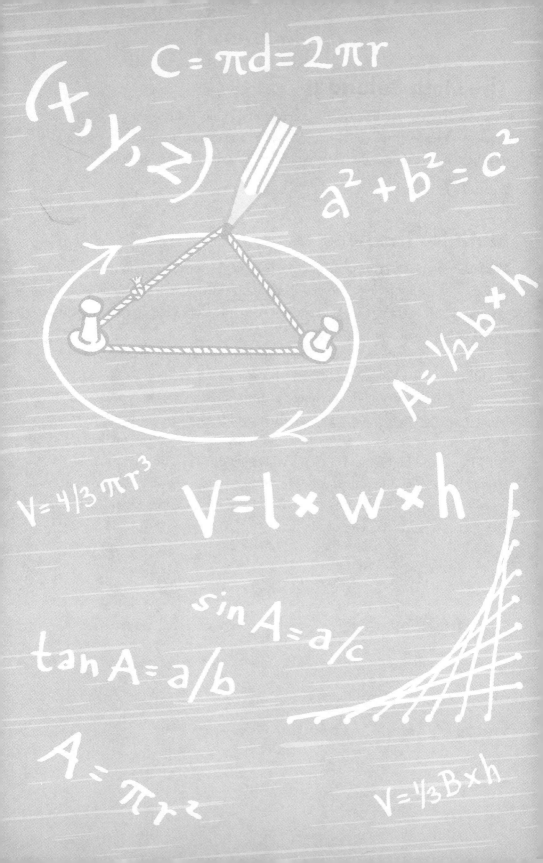

Glossary

acute triangle: A triangle with all three angles less than 90 degrees.

adjacent side: The length of a side of a triangle next to the angle.

angle: A corner formed by two lines extending from the same point.

arc: A continuous portion of a curved line.

area: The surface inside a figure or shape.

caliper: A tool with two adjustable legs used to measure diameter.

central angle: Any angle formed by the center of the circle and two radii.

central angle theorem: Any inscribed angle will be twice the central angle.

chord: A straight line joining two points on a circle.

circle: A line segment that is curved so that its ends meet and every point on the line is equally far away from a single point inside.

circumference: The distance measured along the outside of a circle.

clinometer: A tool used to measure angles of elevation.

compass: An instrument for drawing circles.

concentric circles: Circles with a common center.

cone (conic): A shape created by rotating a right angle about one of its legs

congruent: Equal, or having the same size and shape.

cosine: The length of the adjacent side of a right triangle divided by the length of the hypotenuse.

cube (cubic): Having the three-dimensional form of a cube.

cylinder: A geometric shape made of two parallel circles and a curved surface completely connecting their borders.

derivative: A mathematical concept used to show the rate of change.

diameter: A line that goes through the center of a circle from outside edge to outside edge.

displacement: A vector that tells you how the position of an object has changed.

ellipse: An oval shape.

equilateral triangle: A triangle with three equal sides and three equal angles.

foci: One of the two points within an ellipse, the sum of whose distances from any point on the ellipse is constant.

graphing: To represent by or plot on a graph, as in equations.

hyperbola: A curve formed by the intersection of a double right circular cone with a plane that cuts both halves of the cone.

hypotenuse: The side of a right triangle that is opposite the 90-degree angle.

inscribed angle: Any angle that is created by three points on the circumference of a circle.

intersecting lines: Two nonparallel lines that only can intersect at one point.

isosceles triangle: A triangle with two equal-length sides.

line: A shape with only one dimension: length. A line extends an infinite distance.

line segment: A portion of a line between two points.

line of symmetry: A line of a polygon where the folded sides are equal.

linear: A straight line, involving a single dimension.

major axis: The axis passing through the foci of an ellipse.

midsegment theorem: A midsegment connecting two sides of a triangle is parallel to the third side and half as long.

minor axis: The chord of an ellipse passing through the center, and perpendicular to the major axis.

obtuse triangle: A triangle with one angle greater than 90 degrees.

opposite side: The height of a triangle.

parabola: A curve formed by the intersection of a cone with a plane parallel to a straight line in its surface (a bowl shape)

parallel: Two lines that never intersect; the lines will be an equal distance apart.

parallelogram: A quadrilateral with two sets of equal sides and two sets of equal angles.

pentagon: A shape with five angles and five sides.

perimeter: The boundary of a shape or area.

perpendicular: At a 90-degree angle.

plane: A flat surface that extends forever.

polygon: A closed shape composed of straight lines.

Pythagorean theorem: The sum of the square of each leg of a right triangle is equal to the square of the hypotenuse.

quadrant: Any of the four quarters into which something is divided by lines that intersect each other at right angles.

quadrilateral: Any four-sided shape.

radian: The arc length of the equivalent length of one radius on the outside edge of a circle.

radius (radii): A line from the edge of a circle to the center.

rectangle: A four-sided closed shape with four 90-degree angles.

rectangular prism: A three-dimensional object with six rectangular faces.

resultants: Derived from something else.

rhombus: A quadrilateral with four equal-length sides and equal opposite angles.

right triangle: A triangle that contains one 90-degree angle.

scalene triangle: A triangle with three unequal sides.

section: A part set off by cutting or separating it from the whole.

segment: The finite part of a line between two points in the line.

semicircle: Half of a circle.

similar triangles: Triangles that have exactly the same shape, but are different sizes.

sine: The length of the opposite side of a right triangle divided by the length of the hypotenuse.

slope: The steepness of a line, calculated by dividing its rise by its run.

square: A quadrilateral with four equal sides and four 90-degree angles.

surveying: A branch of mathematics concerned with measuring physical distance.

tangent: The length of the opposite side of a right triangle divided by the length of the adjacent side.

tangram: A Chinese puzzle made by cutting a square into five triangles, a square, and a rhomboid that are capable of being recombined into many different figures.

tessellation: An arrangement of shapes closely fitted together in a repeating pattern.

theorem: In geometry, it is a proven fact. For example, squares have four equal sides and four equal angles.

translation: A geometric transformation that moves every point of a figure by the same distance in a given direction.

trapezoid: A quadrilateral with one set of parallel sides.

triangle: Any three-sided, closed shape.

trigonometry: The study of angles.

unit circle: A circle with a radius of one.

vector: A quantity that is usually represented by a line segment with the given direction and with a length representing magnitude.

vertex (vertices): A point at which two segments of a polygon meet.

vertical angle theorem: Two vertical angles are congruent.

volume: The amount of space a three-dimensional object takes up.

x-component: The part of a vector that points in the same direction as the x-axis.

y-component: The part of a vector that points in the same direction as the y-axis.

y-intercept: The point where a line crosses the y-axis

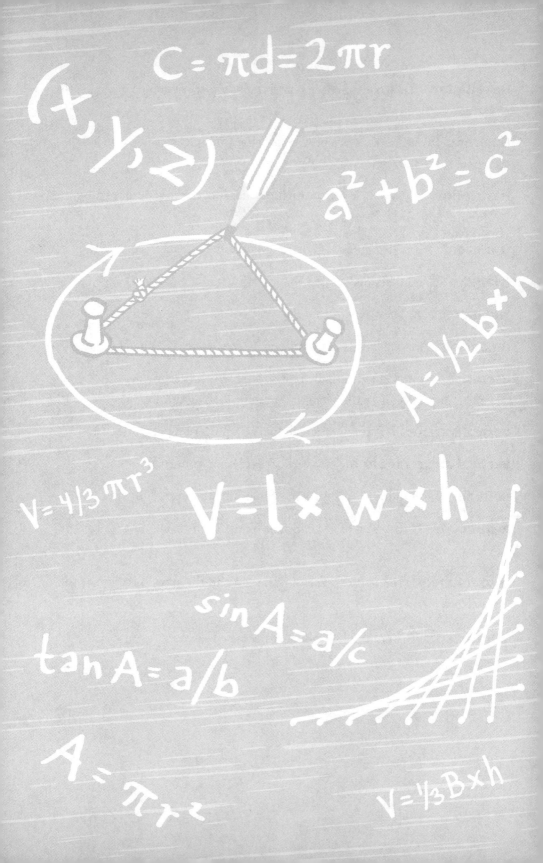

Solutions

T Puzzle (pages 149-154)

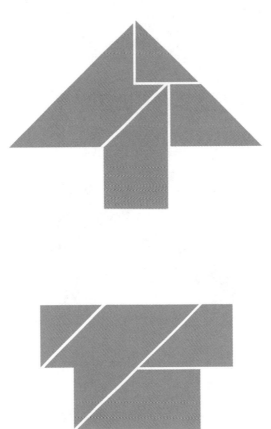

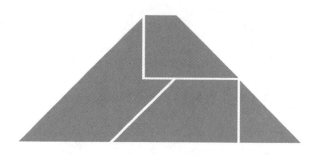

Tangram (pages 154-158)

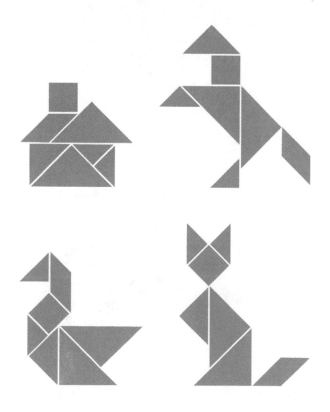

Also available from Chicago Review Press

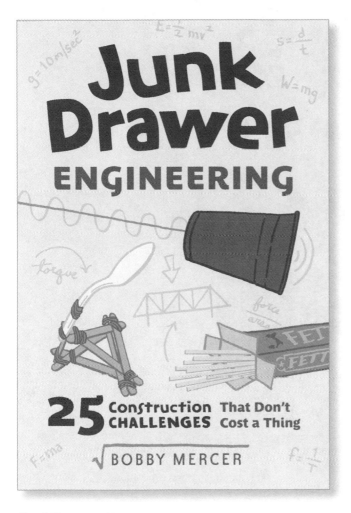

Junk Drawer Engineering
50 Construction Challenges That Don't Cost a Thing
by Bobby Mercer

230 B/W Photos

"The compilation and suggested modifications for youngsters with different backgrounds and skill sets make this particularly welcome for science teachers as well as young learners.... Hours of fun for STEM-inclined kids, parents, caregivers, and teachers." —*Kirkus Reviews*

Trade Paper • 224 pages • ISBN: 978-1-61373-716-3 • $14.99 (CAN $19.99) • Ages 9 and up

Junk Drawer Chemistry
50 Awesome Experiments That Don't Cost a Thing
by Bobby Mercer

230 B/W Photos

"Very highly recommended for family, school, and community library instructional reference collections." —*Midwest Book Review*

Trade Paper, 208 Pages • ISBN: 978-1-61374-920-3 • $14.95 (CAN $17.95) • Ages 9 and up

Junk Drawer Physics
50 Awesome Experiments That Don't Cost a Thing
by Bobby Mercer

230 B/W photos

"More than enough to keep scientifically curious kids busy on rainy days."
—*Publishers Weekly*

Trade Paper, 208 pages • ISBN: 978-1-61374-920-3 • $14.95 (CAN $17.95) • Ages 9 and up